TEACHING ENGLISH IN THE WORKPLACE

Mary Ellen Belfiore
Barbara Burnaby

Pippin Publishing
OISE Press

Pippin Publishing Limited
481 University Avenue
Toronto, Ontario
M5G 2E9

OISE Press, Inc.
The Ontario Institute for Studies in Education
252 Bloor Street West
Toronto, Ontario
M5S 1V6

The publishers wish to acknowledge a contribution from the Ontario Training Adjustment Board, Literacy Branch in the publication of this work.

Chapter 9, "Conducting an Organizational Needs Assessment," by Sue (Waugh) Folinsbee is adapted with permission from "How to Assess Organizational Needs and Requirements" by Sue (Waugh) Folinsbee, which first appeared in *Basic Skills for the Workplace* (M.C. Taylor, G.R. Lewe & J.A. Draper, Eds.). Toronto: Culture Concepts, 1991.

Chapter 12, "Clear Language Documents for the Workplace," by Corinna Frattini is adapted with permission from *Clear Lines: How to Compose and Design Clear Language Documents for the Workplace* by Gordon Nore, which was produced by Learning in the Workplace, Frontier College, Toronto, 1991.

Designed by John Zehethofer
Edited by Dyanne Rivers
Printed and bound in Canada by Canadian Printco Limited

Canadian Cataloguing in Publication Data

Belfiore, Mary Ellen, 1946-
    Teaching English in the workplace

2nd ed. rev.
Includes bibliographical references.
ISBN 0-88751-063-9 (Pippin) ISBN 0-7744-0422-1 (OISE)

1. English language - Study and teaching as a second language (Continuing education).* 2. Working class - Education. I. Burnaby, Barbara J., 1943- II. Ontario Institute for Studies in Education III. Title.

PE1128.A2B45 1995   428'.0071'5   C95-930755-9

ISBN (Pippin) 0-88751-063-9
ISBN (OISE Press) 0-7744-0422-1
10 9 8 7 6 5 4 3 2 1

We would like to acknowledge the many educators, employers and union members who have contributed to the development of workplace education in Canada. Their ideas, determination, energy and vision are transforming our workplaces into centres of work and learning.

For their contributions to this revised and expanded edition of *Teaching English in the Workplace*, we would like to thank in particular Kathleen Flanagan, Virginia Sauvé, Sue Folinsbee, Florence Guy, Kristine Copkov, Marni Johnson, Bridgid Kelso, Valerie Hickey, Julie Finger and Richard Bingham.

Our thanks again to our colleagues who contributed to the first edition—Virginia Sauvé, Jill Bell and Sheila Applebaum—the teachers and classes who were visited and the readers of the first draft for the original edition.

Contents

Introduction

WHO IS THIS BOOK FOR?

This book was written primarily for English as a second language teachers who are preparing to meet the challenge of teaching ESL in the workplace. The focus is on the important role they play in establishing and implementing workplace language programs. We hope, however, that other players, such as organizational managers, union representatives, workplace program co-ordinators and ESL administrators, will also find this book useful in developing an understanding of the process involved, and the importance and scope of the roles of all the key players. In addition, people who teach content other than ESL in the workplace, especially adult basic education, may find the material useful, not only because many of the ideas presented here may apply to their situations but also because it may help clarify the unique features that distinguish ESL programs from others.

WHAT IS THIS BOOK FOR?

The aim of *Teaching English in the Workplace* is to provide ESL teachers with a basic orientation to the workplace program. Because it assumes that teachers have at least some previous knowledge of ESL methods, it is not an introduction to teaching ESL. We have, however, tried to make few assumptions and to lay out, through examples as much as through explanation, what may be involved. As a result, this book does not present a detailed "how to" of workplace language education, such as would be described in a curriculum, but rather outlines practices and principles that can apply to a variety of learners in a variety of workplace settings.

One area that we have left as broad as possible is the form workplace language programs may take. The book addresses ESL teaching and learning for employed people whose first language is not English, conducted at or in some significant way connected to a worksite. It recognizes that learners' education levels in their home language often bear little relationship to the jobs they are employed to do. In addition, their oral and written English skills may be at different stages of development, no matter what their education. As a result, we have tried to consider programs for a range of learners, from those with limited literacy in their first language and those employed at unskilled and semi-skilled work, to those with high levels of education working in skilled occupations.

Workplace programs can take many forms and, as workplace education and training programs continue to evolve, the distinctions among areas such as ESL, vocational and trades training, in-service training, adult basic education, labour education, immigrant orientation and others are blurring. For the purposes of this book, we have assumed that a basic constellation of players, such as sponsors, educational administrators, teachers and learners, will be more or less constant across programs, although other kinds of programs are possible. Although all our examples are drawn from Canadian programs, we do not deal with issues of policy or government funding. As a result, we believe that the principles outlined in this book can be applied in most industrialized countries.

THE FIRST EDITION

The first edition of this book, published in 1984, was one of several related books of guidance for ESL teachers that came out of the Modern Language Centre at the Ontario Institute for Studies in Education. Two others were *A Handbook for ESL Literacy* (J. Bell and B. Burnaby) and *Teaching Multilevel Classes in ESL* (J. Bell). These other books focused on some of the new and challenging ESL situations that were beginning to develop. At that time, ESL teachers in North America were coming to grips with a learner population that was becoming much more varied in terms of education levels, race, first language and life experiences. Providing ESL education to employed workers on the worksite was relatively new and fairly uncommon. The content of the first edition of this book was an earlier version of what is Chapters 2 to 8 in the current edition. Most of the examples in the first edition were drawn from Ontario because that was where most of the programs existed at the time.

CHANGES IN CONTEXT OVER THE PAST DECADE

Since then, the context of workplace language programs has changed dramatically. The growth of technology, the globalization of national economies and the increasing relative size of the service sector in the economies of industrialized nations have altered the face of employment. All levels of government, as well as many organizations in the private sector, are emphasizing productivity, downsizing, information technology, working smarter and teamwork. These initiatives are reflected in a largely revamped approach to training, a recognition of the importance of lifelong learning, and the readiness of management in many organizations to take responsibility for developing skills at every level.

This shift in emphasis has had a major impact on the kinds of jobs available to immigrants with limited English skills; many jobs that required minimal communication no longer exist and most others involve increasing demands for effective communication. The Canadian and United States governments have recognized the need to pay attention to and develop the literacy skills in English (and, in Canada, French) of a significant portion of the population, mostly native born. In addition, Canada raised its immigration quotas in the early 1990s to fill the population gap left at the end of the "baby boom" years. There is, as well, a growing focus on social justice issues, especially those relating to women and racial and ethnic minorities.

The obvious effect of these conditions on workplace ESL education has been an expansion in the number of programs—more where before there were some and new ones in areas where a decade ago there were none. The perspective on these programs has also changed. For example, the Ontario government used to encourage English in the workplace programs. In the late 1980s, however, it began promoting multiculturalism in the workplace programs. This represented a philosophical shift from a policy directed only at changing the behaviour of non-English-speaking immigrants to conform to English linguistic norms to a policy that emphasizes that all employees need to change in some ways in order to create effective and respectful communication in a multicultural organization.

In addition, the number and variety of players have greatly increased. Not only have more managers become involved, but unions have also taken an active role. As for the delivery agencies, government policies, in Canada and the U.S. at least, have both allowed and forced a wide range of public and private educational institutions and non-governmental organizations to take part. The result has been that virtually every ESL workplace program involves at least two partners, each of whom brings to the project unique skills, knowledge, values, prejudices, issues and problems. When the major stakeholders in an organization have an interest in a project and when their various interests are successfully negotiated, the program that results can be a realistic, holistic and synergistic improvement in workplace communications that satisfies everyone involved.

THE REVISED EDITION

In the revised edition of *Teaching English in the Workplace*, we wanted both to update the material from the first edition and to add discussion of matters that have come to the fore since 1984. On reviewing the material from the first edition in light of current conditions in workplace education, we found that the principles and methods remained fundamentally relevant. However, our examples were out-of-date and too narrow in a number of ways. Therefore, Mary Ellen Belfiore rewrote the original chapters dealing with the participants, negotiations, needs analysis, designing a syllabus, developing materials, establishing classroom sequences, and assessment and evaluation. They appear as Chapters 2 to 8 in this book. Many of the examples are new and are drawn from sites across the country. In compiling these, we are indebted to many workplace teachers and co-ordinators for supplying samples of their work as well as advice about our principles and priorities.

One specific aspect of these chapters has been considerably changed. In the first edition, we focused mainly on workers in unskilled and semi-skilled jobs and assumed that they had only limited education and proficiency in English. In the rewritten chapters, the needs and interests of a broader spectrum of learners are considered—from those with low levels of literacy in their first language to those with high levels of education, and from those who work at unskilled jobs to those who do complex, communication-centred work. In addition, some of the examples have been specifically chosen to demonstrate how social justice issues, especially anti-racist strategies, are an important part of workplace education.

Just as we wanted to include examples and ideas provided by the many excellent workplace education specialists in Chapters 2 to 8 of the revised edition, we also wanted to highlight the expertise of our colleagues with respect to certain issues and practices. Therefore, we commissioned six new chapters for this edition. Two of them provide an extended discussion and a specific case description, one of a formative program evaluation (Angela Gillis, Chapter 13) and the other of a drop-in learning unit at a British Columbia sawmill (Mary Ellen Belfiore interviewing Christina Pikios, Chapter 11). Two more are concerned with specific issues: Kathleen Flanagan interviewed a number of workplace educators about anti-racist strategies (Chapter 10) and Corinna Frattini describes concepts of clear language, which places the onus on the writer to make the message straightforward and easy-to-read (Chapter 12). As well, Sue (Waugh) Folinsbee outlines in detail how to conduct a needs assessment (Chapter 9), and Virginia Sauvé, who runs a private company in Edmonton that offers, among other things, English in the workplace programs for employers, introduces the book by relating the importance of connecting with learners on a human level in light of her sense of the pervasiveness of social justice matters (Chapter 1).

We have also included a listing of helpful resources—both classroom materials and books and articles of interest to workplace teachers. While materials produced in Toronto are strongly represented here, this isn't intended to suggest that these materials represent everything that is available across the continent. A great deal of resource material is produced by school boards, colleges, municipalities, local agencies, and the like. Because it is not published by commercial houses, it is difficult to find a comprehensive listing of what is available. Workplace teachers and others are encouraged to ask around in their own communities to see what has been produced.

In gathering the material for this edition, we have drawn from the work of many skilled, experienced and insightful people. We hope that professionals in workplace language education see this book as a reflection of their best practice in Canada. Of course, we take full responsibility for any misrepresentations we may have made.

A final point. The events and profiles of learners and others that appear throughout the text may be composite pictures. As a result, they do not necessarily reflect the complete experiences of a single learner, administrator, teacher or sponsor.

Barbara Burnaby
Toronto, 1995

CHAPTER 1 # Reflections on Teaching English in the Workplace

by Virginia Sauvé

The story that follows is true. It is a lived moment in the real world of workplace teaching, a heart-to-heart reflection on a moment in time, written from the perspective of the day it happened. I hope it affords you an "experience" of teaching English in the workplace and sets the stage for the many fine ideas presented in this book.

. . . .

This morning, I met with the co-ordinator of our English in the workplace programs. We were discussing the need to completely revisit our conceptual frameworks for programs in the face of the rapidly shrinking budgets and shifting priorities in many workplaces today. Even those who want to support workplace programs are finding it hard to justify budgets and release time for workers to attend.

During the discussion, one class in a food-processing industry came up. The co-ordinator expressed the anguish she had felt when she interviewed some of the students for the final evaluation and each unloaded up to $1\frac{1}{2}$ hours of the pain and suffering in their lives.

"I'm no therapist," she said, "but how could I cut them off when they needed so desperately to be heard? And, having heard them, how could I then in conscience proceed to ask, 'And what did you learn in the English classes?'"

Her comments resonated with several experiences I have had lately: teaching a class of learners with special needs in our large program in a garment factory, visiting a group of hospital workers fearful of losing their jobs and being unable to find another, listening to teacher after teacher speak of the need for transitional skills in an increasingly insecure workplace. There seemed to be a connection among all these experiences, but I was not sure what it was.

The co-ordinator and I continued our conversation as we were preparing a proposal to extend the program in the food-processing plant. We knew that we were losing our competitive edge for, although the quality of our programs doesn't seem to be in dispute, the cost is. What can we cut? How can we ensure that the cuts do not seriously impair our ability to provide quality learning experiences for these learners? Why is it that some learners don't appear to have learned much even though they have been in the program for some time? Should these learners be given more classes when there are others who need them and have not had the chance to attend? And what about the supervisors telling the women who can and cannot participate? What is the meaning of this kind of power and what are the implications for our classes? I listened to the co-ordinator's concerns and then we called in the teacher and spoke with her. I decided to visit the class.

After driving to the north end of the city, I entered the industrial area where the plant is located and searched for a parking place as there were none left on the factory lot. I was lucky. I parked across the road in a two-hour zone, wondering where the women workers parked when they had to stay all day. I walked somewhat fearfully on the busy four-lane roadway because the snowdrifts were piled high and the sidewalks had not been cleared. How strange this world of snow and cold must be for these women from Vietnam and Cambodia!

As I entered the small classroom, about 10 faces eyed me curiously, some looking resentful at the interruption and others looking happy and expectant. I felt out of place in my street clothes as all of them wore white gowns over their clothes and hairnets over their shiny black hair.

As they studied me, I studied them, thinking of the rapidly moving assembly lines that govern their rate of work. I could tell they were the shift getting ready to go on because they didn't look tired, as they do when they are coming off a full shift. I understood why some of the faces looked impatient with my presence. I was, after all, an intruder and I knew from previous experience that, for many of them, this time could well represent the only moments of peace and laughter in the day. Like so many immigrant women in entry-level jobs, they were working in jobs they did not like, for people whom they felt were unfair and condescending, for wages that made it barely worthwhile. Then, when they left the plant, some went to part-time cleaning jobs, while others cooked and cleaned at home and did what every mother does to ensure that her children are ready for school the next day. I could not ask my questions outright. I had to earn that privilege.

So, we chatted. I asked their names, where they were from and how long they had been in Canada. They had obviously been asked these questions many times before and could answer without fearing the embarrassment of making a mistake. I explained that I was there to learn more about what they need in future programs. Then, I invited them to ask me questions. After a short period of giggles and silence, in which we all exchanged very important smiles of patience and understanding, respect and acceptance, someone finally said, "Where do you live?"

"Near the university," I said, as some nodded to indicate their comprehension. "On the south side." For a few more, the light of understanding dawned. Then someone asked if I had children.

"Yes," I said, "I had four children, a son and three daughters, but my son was killed in an accident when he was 17." Most looked sympathetic, a couple interpreted for those who had not understood, and a couple expressed their sorrow.

Then, one of them pointed to the woman next to me and said, "She lose five children, whole family. She only one left. Pol Pot."

Yet another woman fought back the tears welling in her own eyes and I saw the anxiety rising around the table. I waited a respectful moment to show my sorrow for her pain, then suggested that we not talk about Pol Pot anymore. They all responded with a sigh of relief and invited me to a party they were having on Thursday.

At this point, I thought to myself, we have shared something. We have found a little common ground. I can almost ask them what I really need to know, but not quite. So I asked them how they liked Canada and what was different. They mentioned the safe things: people look different; people eat different foods.

"Are people friendly here?" I asked.

"Oh yes," they said.

"Good," I replied. "You are lucky."

At this, the teacher asked, "What about at the factory? Are people friendly here?"

Some said yes, others were silent. Then one woman said, "Sometimes not fair."

At this point, the whole thing opened up and stories began to pour out as fast as there was an opening.

"I work here four half years. I go Hong Kong two months holiday. I come back. My supervisor say I go Hong Kong, no English classes. Not fair."

Another said, "I work here seven years. This my first English class. (We have been in the factory for three years with English classes). No good. Supervisor say no good learn English. Say we speak too much English, we complain too much."

Everyone then echoed this sentiment. Suddenly, I understood what I had not in my conversation with the co-ordinator in the morning; namely, the reason the supervisors' decisions about who could—and could not—come to classes appeared to be so arbitrary and political. The reality for these women was that there were many problems and a lot of these appeared to be rooted in the power the supervisors had over their lives. The supervisors, by the way, spoke their language and were men.

At this point, I remembered the special classes we had held for two of the supervisors and our frustration over the fact that their English was fossilized and difficult to understand because of serious pronunciation problems.

The instructor's next comment seemed almost unnecessary: "The supervisors do not want the women to speak more English than they do and they do not want them to be able to complain."

I asked, "If your supervisor says you can't take the English class again, could you go to the plant manager and tell him you want to come? Would that be a problem?"

"Big problem!" they all said. One woman told a story of getting nowhere in making a request of her supervisor and going upstairs to ask the boss. When she returned, she was told that if she had a problem she was to go only to the supervisor and that if she ever went over his head again, she would be fired. (She did not use these words but her gestures and words certainly painted the picture very clearly.)

I sat stunned at the contradictions educators face in this context, and at the contradictions faced by the women themselves. On the one hand, they told me, they needed English to understand and express their rights, to stand up for themselves, and to have choices. On the other hand, their first need was to survive and that meant having a job. We all knew that the entire plant workforce could quit tomorrow and be replaced immediately by people willing to put up with whatever was dished out.

At this point, four of the women were crying, a pretty clear sign of the degree of their common distress. As they wiped their eyes, we all started to laugh at ourselves. The futility of crying did indeed strike a tragically humorous chord. We looked at our watches, expressed our happiness at meeting one another, and prepared to leave—but not before the woman who had lost all her children and all her extended family reached out and reminded me to be sure to come to their party on Thursday, a party to which they had decided not to invite the supervisors.

I left the small building, dodged the traffic and scrambled over the huge windrows of snow cleared by the plows to make way for the traffic that passes by that factory every day, drivers totally oblivious to the lives of those who pack the food their children place in their lunchboxes. And I gave thanks for the small window of understanding I had been privileged to share that afternoon. And last, I bowed my head in respect for the courage, the determination and the dignity of these women who are willing to suffer their humiliation and frustration in silence so that their own children can wear Doc Martens, take piano lessons and study dentistry, medicine and law at the university.

Now, I sit at my computer in my home that is finally paid for this year and wonder how the woman who left the class early is doing: she received an emergency phone call telling her that the water pipes had burst in the extreme cold, and her basement apartment was flooded. Her sister, who speaks no English, was there alone with her child, and they were terrified at the volume of water that had risen to the level of bottom drawers of clothing and bottom shelves of food. While she bails buckets of water, I sip my tea and wonder at the meaning of teaching English in the workplace.

· · · · · · · · · · ·

We have a choice when we teach. We can teach purely from the head or we can teach also from the heart. Part of me wished I had gone with that woman who had left early to bail out her apartment. And I suddenly remembered the time the same thing happened to me. It was an immigrant woman who helped me bail out my basement for many long, hard hours.

We have many choices. We can teach to support the status quo we find in various workplaces—the language of production, protocol and procedure that is certainly necessary and certainly what management expects. Or we can teach this—and more. We can walk the tightrope that risks listening to the truth although, at any moment, a supervisor could come through the door and wonder what is going on. In taking this chance, we assume a tremendous responsibility, for we risk breaking the trust that allows us to be there in the first place and, in so doing, we risk destroying the only chance these workers may have to find the voices that will enable them to recognize and choose what is best for their own lives and the lives of their families.

What we clearly have no right to do is to act in ways that take away the right and ability of participants to make their own decisions. We must be quiet when we would rather not. We must question our own motives and our own understandings and ask ourselves again and again which decisions are ours to make and which are not.

Are all workplaces unjust? Of course not. But the reality of life in Canada for immigrant workers is often a reality that is very foreign to many of us. I am amazed at the current outcry against our immigration policies. I am amazed at the ignorance from which this outcry springs and at the irony present within it, for the very people who protest and blame our immigrants for all the social and economic problems of the country are the same people who benefit from those who work at wages others would not accept, doing jobs they would not do in working conditions that some of us could only call Draconian.

Those of us who teach in workplace programs have our eyes opened, if we are at all willing to see, and with this seeing comes a responsibility to understand, to inform and to take a stand in a way that may affect our own lives but must not take away from the workers their rights to determine the course of their own lives within the inevitable parameters of ability and circumstance.

Having worked in a variety of workplace programs, some for excellent employers and some for questionable ones, I can say with all honesty that I believe that questions of social justice will not much longer go unasked. As the numbers of unemployed increase and the fear of being unemployed increases even more, as the gap between rich and poor widens in our country and as provinces like Alberta kill, in months, social programs that took decades to build, we will see growing intolerance and shrinking opportunities for immigrant workers to stand up for their limited rights.

This leaves those of us who work with these learners to make some very uncomfortable decisions about the parameters of curriculum in practice. What language do we teach? To what point can we advocate for those who have no voice without jeopardizing the well-being of those on whose behalf we would advocate? At what point do we refuse to cut our budgets any more because we are beginning to exploit our own workers (the teachers and administrators who work with these learners)? To what extent and in what manner are we obliged to work with employers to develop their understanding of the issues faced by their immigrant workers? In what ways can we develop materials that go beyond the daily functional language and literacy needs of learners to provide the human support needed to survive in a society that can be racist and unjust in its treatment of various peoples? At what point can we no longer stretch our own energy and time without jeopardizing our health and the well-being of our own families?

Long-term workplace educators, in my experience, are often among the most committed, the most aware, and the most compassionate of ESL personnel because, if they were not, they would not be able to deal with the spartan working conditions of most workplace sites, not to mention the part-time nature of the work, the additional costs such as transportation, and the stress of knowing that there are conditions we can do nothing about even when we know they are not right.

Yet, despite the challenges, there is an enormous sense that we are privileged to see our society from a totally different perspective and a great sense of fulfilment in knowing that what little we can do in the few precious hours we have with these learners may make the difference one person needs to change her or his life.

We have an obligation to be aware of the changes in our society and how they will affect the immigrant workers with whom we work. We need to question and question again the role we play in our educational programs: can we afford to be only delivery-persons bringing packages of learning to designated "target" groups? Or, would we be better to see ourselves as agents of change, working with employers and employees alike to better the whole communicative network in the work environment? Or, should we take the stance of enablers in partnership with learners?

There is no single answer and certainly no easy answer. Rather, we are each faced with contexts—of time, space and circumstance. In these contexts, we have choices, as individual teachers, as administrators, as teacher-educators. For me, the challenge is to make responsible, informed choices, which I can look back on 20 years later and know, beyond a shadow of a doubt, that I did the best I could.

If I have any words of advice for new educators to this field, they are: Try to listen for that still small voice of intuition as you make decisions. If something does not feel right, it probably isn't. If you have the feeling that something is not being said, it probably isn't. Listen to the learners and they will be your teachers, for only when we have learned to listen do we have the right to speak; only when we have learned to learn can we possibly hope to teach. And last, do not underestimate the value of hope. For, in every situation that seems hopeless, there is something to celebrate, something on which to build the hope that tomorrow does not have to be like today.

As teachers, we have a tendency to see what learners do not know. But we will not succeed in connecting with learners until we recognize and acknowledge each individual for whom he or she is and what he or she knows! Until this connection is made, how can we possibly imagine that we have anything to teach the Other? We must find our common ground and, upon that ground, we can create new and better tomorrows.

CHAPTER 2 English in the Workplace: The Participants

A teacher in the textile industry commented, "It's the nature of our job to be part of the life of the factory." This comment captures the dynamic between workplace and classroom that distinguishes our work as ESL teachers in the workplace. We join a team of participants and partners that includes the learners, their company and union, the educational institution, community agencies and ourselves. In this chapter, we'll look first look at how and why employers and unions get involved, then at who the learners are and why they come to class and, finally, at the link between the educational institution and our role as teachers in the workplace.

RECOGNIZING COMMUNICATION PROBLEMS

As the following examples show, English in the workplace classes exist because the management, the union or the workers have recognized a communication problem.

A bank supervisor in the statistical section asked a staff member to make a short presentation on the recent changes in her job. Although she agreed readily, her extreme nervousness during the presentation made her audience uncomfortable. When a communications course was offered at her bank, she requested that "making presentations" be one of its primary goals.

A small city hospital changed its meal service procedure to offer a more restaurant-like atmosphere. The catering staff would now have to read the menu order forms and serve each patient individually. When managers found that several employees were not able to read the forms, they contacted a local board of education for assistance.

The workplace program offered was open to all employees and the resulting classes also included nurses' aides and orderlies.

A union local at a textile plant tried to recruit rank-and-file members for shop steward training. When the recruitment drive did not produce a healthy number of trainees, officials took a closer look at the language background and needs of their members. Most of their members had not received formal ESL training in Canada and used their native languages at work to communicate with their peers. Without a good command of English, they did not feel confident enough to handle training or to deal with union issues on a daily basis.

The resulting workplace course was held in the union hall. The union's initiative to recruit and train shop stewards was delayed in favour of an ESL course that used union-oriented content to help rank-and-file members develop language skills and raise their confidence in communicating with others.

Aurelia's six-year-old daughter needed extra attention at school because of her allergy problems. Because her daughter's previous teacher had been able to speak Portuguese, Aurelia had no trouble talking to her in her native language about the doctor's orders, medication, warnings, etc. But her next teacher could not speak Portuguese, and Aurelia felt uncomfortable about communicating with her through an interpreter.

A workplace course for housekeepers had been running for two months at the hospital where Aurelia worked. Although her coworkers had urged her to sign up when it began, she had felt at that time that she couldn't stay for an extra hour after work. She did register for the following session with a definite purpose and commitment to learning English.

As these examples indicate, the specific incidents that highlight the need for an ESL program may vary; nevertheless, in most cases, communication problems related directly to the workplace or to life in the community are the common trigger.

RATIONALE: THE VIEWS OF MANAGEMENT AND UNIONS

In the bank example mentioned earlier, management clearly linked communication problems with the quality of service being offered. In other cases, new procedures—often involving the introduction of new technology—may highlight an immediate need for specific language skills. In many instances though, the connection with communication skills is not so evident. For example, it may take several major accidents before management realizes that employees are not able to fully understand health and safety regulations, follow instructions or ask questions about safety measures.

Management does not usually associate the time and money factors involved in productivity with effective communication. For instance, unnecessary time may be spent using translators to relay messages between employees and supervisors. Expensive materials can be wasted if workers do not understand spoken or written instructions. Difficulty in recruiting supervisory staff internally may also be linked to the language proficiency of employees who are better-than-average at their own jobs but are not confident that they can handle the oral and written language demands of the supervisory level.

As in the example cited earlier, unions may view a workplace course as a first step in involving the members in continuing training for union positions. But more often, the union offers the course either independently or jointly with management to provide a learning environment in which communication skills can be developed in a labour context with content focusing on workers' rights and procedures for solving work-related problems. For instance, health and safety issues discussed in class from a labour perspective would emphasize the employer's responsibilities as well as those of the workers. Discussions like this would also teach learners to use the procedures for reporting and changing an unsafe worksite.

As a result of the emphasis on retraining in many industries, unions have begun to view workplace classes as part of the larger issue of job security. Workers are able to take advantage of retraining only if their language proficiency level can meet the demands of the training programs. Upgrading skills or learning new ones enables union members to keep pace with the changes in their workplace. Communication skills are also central to full participation at membership meetings, in committees and other union activities. In many union-sponsored classes, building self-confidence and self-esteem is the starting point for participation.

WHO ARE THE LEARNERS?

Learners in workplace ESL classes are usually adults with English as their second language or dialect. They come from a wide variety of backgrounds and include French-speaking Canadians. They can be in their early 20s and just entering the workforce or people within a few years of retirement who have finally found the right opportunity to learn. A large percentage are women who have not been able to attend language classes because of work schedules, home responsibilities or cultural barriers that deny women access to continuing education.

For many learners, traditional classroom education may be very much a childhood experience if they have completed only Grade 3 or 4. They may have no experience at all with formal learning in their native language so that pre-literacy training must be the first step. Generally, however, learners in workplace classes have some degree of literacy in their native language; that is, they can read and write in their native language to a greater or lesser degree. But in English, their second or additional language, their literacy levels may be lower. Often, they have survival reading and writing skills in English, but are not functionally literate. Or, they may feel comfortable with the basic reading and writing required in their current jobs, but lack the skills to handle the more sophisticated reading and writing needed to advance to a higher-level job. To help them improve their literacy skills in English, it is important for the teacher to be aware of their degree of familiarity with reading and writing in their native language.

Often, basic level learners can speak and listen better than they can read and write. They may work at unskilled or semi-skilled jobs that don't, at first sight, require them to have extensive communication skills to perform their work. They may avoid English communicative situations whenever possible. They may lack confidence in their ability to learn and to tackle the wider world of communication. But once they take the first step by agreeing to enrol in the course, their open, determined commitment and exposure to a sensitive teaching and learning environment can overcome fear and develop self-assurance.

Satvant is a 30-year-old Punjabi woman who came to Canada five year ago with her husband and two children. Despite her desire to return to India, the family has become more settled every year and Satvant has begun to feel the pressure to "learn Canadian ways." Soon after arriving in Canada, she started working in a small electronics manufacturing firm. For the last three years, she has worked in a large, high-pressure factory as a sewing machine operator.

During the interview for the workplace class, she was confident and able to interact quite well orally. With help from a friend, she filled in the written questionnaire adequately and was placed in the most advanced of the three classes running in the factory. After three days of instruction, she was finally forced by frustration and determination to announce: "I can't read. Please, I want to." From this crucial request came a new emphasis on literacy training, which prepared her for her first big challenge. She had always handed her paycheque to her husband who cashed it, gave her $50 and looked after the rest himself. The day Satvant opened her own bank account and deposited her salary marked her first tangible success in dealing independently with the demands of a literate society.

Pui Kwan's afternoon and evening shift busing in the city's largest hotel was a far cry from her responsibility as a cook and businessperson in Hong Kong. At 28, she seemed to be falling far behind the goals she wanted to achieve in the food service industry. Managers insisted that she attend the workplace English classes because they found her troublesome, disruptive and insensitive to customers' needs. Her English, they said, was "loud and terrible."

The teacher found Pui Kwan bright and perceptive, though somewhat disruptive in class at times. Her good listening skills were offset by real problems in oral communication, especially pronunciation. Pui Kwan was pregnant in a fast-moving job, and had to cope with family problems as well as reprimands from her supervisor at work. It wasn't surprising that sometimes she just "refused to comprehend." In class, Pui Kwan commanded attention by clowning or exercising her charismatic qualities. Her Chinese-speaking peers were very supportive and understanding, though somewhat cautious. They felt that management had adopted a stereotypical view of all Chinese workers in the hotel based on Pui Kwan's behaviour.

One day in class, Pui Kwan's abrupt request to work specifically with the teacher and not with the aide was acknowledged by the teacher who provided concentrated and sensitive assistance at that moment. A dramatic turning point!

Trust was established and Pui Kwan soon gained self-confidence and improved her ability to express herself orally.

Jean is a telephone data recorder for a specialized evaluation project with a major accounting firm. Bilingual in French and English, he is a black Québécois with roots in Haiti and credits from an English-speaking university. He is completely comfortable and competent on the phone in both French and English, but with a recent reorganization of the project, he is now being asked to take on more responsibility in his section. This requires him to take minutes at section meetings, write up brief reports and present bi-weekly progress reports.

When one of his colleagues approached management with the idea of initiating a communications course, Jean supported the suggestion. Two months into the course, he has already tackled the new oral and written demands of his job with success. An unexpected area of investigation for Jean was the racism he experienced in his telephone work. When he commented on a racist incident at work, other colleagues felt impelled to tell their own stories and an exploration of race, culture and language became a strong theme in the course.

Armando is an outdoor worker with the city's transportation system. After 2½ years with the transit company, he's still considered a "new man" on the job so he follows the accepted ways of doing things even though he would sometimes like to take the lead and change them. He often feels that his job is unsafe because he frequently has to work alone without a flagman to warn oncoming traffic of his presence.

With 30 working years ahead of him, a growing family and a job that he is uneasy with, Armando would like to take advantage of the company training courses to secure a safer and higher-paid position. Until now, his jobs in construction in Italy and Canada have not demanded any writing skills. During the 12 years that he's been in Canada, he's developed enough oral skills to talk his way through any situation. Even though he has very little formal education, his reading in English is well beyond the survival level. Before he attended the workplace classes, he depended on his children to help him with writing. He had never really tried to write in English so, with a lot of courage and many apologies for his incomprehensible scrawl, he began to produce words. He keeps looking for new ways to learn more words, to master their spelling and to make meaning on the page. He is a proud adult learner who comes to classes even on his days off and carries his reading and writing exercises with him everywhere he goes.

EDUCATION PROVIDERS

Just as the types of workplace programs have developed and expanded since the mid-1980s, so have the types of education providers. Traditional educational institutions—boards of education, community colleges and universities—are still significant players in providing on-site instruction. They have been joined, however, by independent consultants, small educational businesses and non-traditional adult learning agencies, such as the Open Learning Agency in British Columbia.

Another change is the development and importance of partnerships in mounting and funding workplace education. Providers are often part of a consortium of stakeholders or of an advisory committee. These groups may include representatives of the community, funders and graduates of the program in addition to union or company members or both. Skillplan in British Columbia, which provides workplace education for the construction industry, is an example in which a consortium of organizations is responsible for the project.

MORE THAN TEACHING: THE ROLES OF WORKPLACE TEACHERS

As teachers in the workplace, our job extends well beyond the classroom walls. Because we are in contact with the learners, the sponsors and the educational institution, we provide the link among all the participants in the program. In this key position, it is certainly desirable for us to take on new roles and responsibilities by participating in the initial negotiations, needs analysis, curriculum development and evaluation of programs.

In some workplace programs, the teacher and the co-ordinator (or consultant) share these responsibilities. For instance, a co-ordinator-consultant may assume responsibility for negotiating the contract and doing a needs analysis, then hire a teacher to follow through. Even if we, as teachers, enter at this stage, we are responsible for developing and teaching a course based on the findings of a needs analysis and the results of the negotiations. We are also responsible for building relationships with the sponsors of the course so that we can integrate language development into the working environment and improve overall knowledge and communication in the workplace.

In other programs, teachers are involved in the initial steps, assuming responsibility for carrying out the needs analysis, deciding on the level of the course and who will participate and determining the hours and location of the class. No matter how the roles are divided, we must be aware of all the elements of the process and of their potential effects before we can design a course effectively. At a very general level, for example, we need to know whether the discussions with industry management or the union identified a special need for oral rather than written skills. Did the potential participants in the course express the same needs?

When teaching in the workplace, we may find that our responsibilities increase with each new project. After teaching two or three classes, we may be called upon to take part in the negotiations or needs analysis or prepare a syllabus and materials for other similar projects. Our experience is valuable to people entering the field and those interested in expanding workplace services. We can assume, then, that as our experience grows, so will our responsibilities. The field is exciting and demanding, offering us the opportunity to be part of a team of people engaged in teaching and learning communications skills.

Virginia Sauvé, an experienced workplace teacher from Alberta and the author of the first chapter of this book, has prepared a model in which the educator appears as a consultant specializing in communication. As educators in the workplace environment, we can take on the roles of negotiator and needs analyst, program designer and evaluator in addition to that of classroom teacher. The following diagram, adapted from Sauvé's model, illustrates the extent of our job. More important, it shows that we are called upon to provide expertise in areas not traditionally associated with the classroom but vital to the workplace setting.

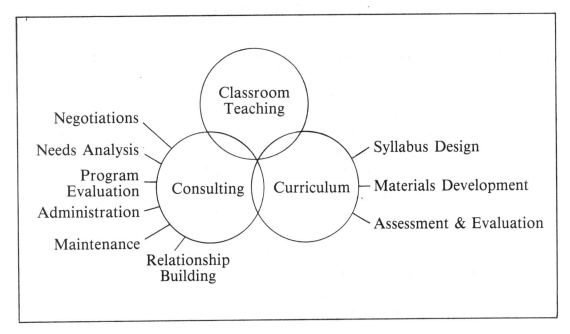

It's worth noting that Sauvé describes her original as a "change agent" model. In it, she distinguishes between project and program: "project" refers to communication within the company itself and "program" refers to issues of specific language course design. For instance, she places the first—and essential—needs analysis within the industry at the project level. The program needs analysis relating to one specific course within the company, however, is placed at the program level.

CHAPTER 3 Conducting Negotiations

When we hear that contract negotiations are taking place, we tend to think of money and improvements in working conditions. Similarly, negotiations involving workplace programs include issues dealing with finances and good teaching and learning conditions. Once the sponsor, whether this is a company or union or both, has recognized the need for improved communication and has contacted a provider of educational services, discussions begin on an appropriate course.

Sponsors usually delegate one employee to be the "contact," the person responsible for the workplace program. In large industries, service institutions and businesses, the management contact is often a member of the human resources or staff development department. In smaller workplaces, the general manager, a department manager or a line supervisor could be the contact. In unions, the service agent, a member of the local executive, the head of the education committee or a shop steward is often the link between the teacher and the rank-and-file membership. These contact people are usually the key players who represent the sponsors during negotiations to set up a workplace program.

The educational providers who deliver the course can be represented by a program co-ordinator, a "lead instructor" (teacher or administrator responsible for a small group of teachers) or the actual teacher of the course. Co-ordinators of workplace programs often do the negotiating themselves without the assistance of a teacher. Because there is often no firm commitment from the company or union at this stage, co-ordinators may be reluctant to hire a teacher. They may be unable to obtain the funds to pay a teacher to participate in the negotiations or feel they do not have enough time to interview and hire a teacher before negotiations begin. The job of negotiating is part of the "consulting" role which is just one aspect of working in our programs.

FINANCING

The financing of workplace education has changed significantly, especially with the recession and the deficit-minded public budgets of the early 1990s. In the early years, the bulk of the financial commitment to cover teaching and administration was met by the public sector, often through school boards and community colleges. Now, the dollars are more often provided through partnerships among government, educational institutions, businesses and unions.

Management, for example, may assume some financial responsibility by offering the course during company time so that employees receive full or partial wages while they are attending. A common formula involves a 50-50 split, whereby employees are paid for half the class time and volunteer their time for the remaining half. In a workplace that has a 4:30 quitting time, for instance, a 3:30-5:30 class might be scheduled. The first hour is paid study time and the final hour is on the workers' own time. Occasionally, employers pay full or partial wages to employees who attend classes after work hours or award bonuses on completion of the course. In one program, management offered financial assistance by paying for an extra teacher to reduce the class size to an 8:1 ratio.

The sponsors may agree to help finance the needs analysis or curriculum development, although this can turn out to be a controversial issue. Some teachers and co-ordinators believe that because the sponsors benefit from the course, they should bear some of these costs. Historically, part-time teachers—the status of most workplace teachers—have been paid only for their contact hours with the class, not for the time they spend developing curriculum, attending staff meetings, conducting evaluations, etc. Some teachers believe that the sponsors should fund their curriculum development work on a set-fee or hourly basis. Others believe that curriculum is too sensitive an area for sponsors to finance directly: if sponsors pay for developing the curriculum, they may wish to control its content, methodology or use. For this reason, some teachers prefer to request additional funds from their educational institution, which they see as a more neutral and responsive body. Sponsors may help to meet immediate classroom needs by providing copying facilities, blackboards, flip charts, cabinets for supplies and materials and perhaps refreshments.

WORKING CONDITIONS

The working conditions that relate to workplace programs should be understood in the broadest sense; that is, the conditions necessary for effective teaching and learning. To establish suitable working conditions, there should be a clear identification of who is involved in the negotiation process, a mutual understanding of why the course is being offered and a good sense of the aims of the negotiations. Aims include setting a contract for the course, establishing the responsibility of each player, and so on.

The first meeting between the sponsor(s) and the workplace consultant not only establishes a working rapport but also outlines the working conditions. A working rapport is based on a mutual understanding of why the course is being offered and how it can best be delivered. The sponsor may have recognized the need for improved communication as a result of a specific incident, but probably does not realize the intricacies of the communication network the employees are required to use, involving both linguistic and social behaviours.

> When the hotel mentioned in the previous chapter requested an English course because the housekeepers could not read the new order forms, management viewed the communication problem in terms of a single reading task. As it turned out, however, the problem involved more than simply reading the form. It also involved using it. In reality, the task required the supervisor and housekeeper to speak to each other, and possibly use even more advanced reading and writing skills. This simple task involved a network of contacts— with supervisory staff, laundry staff, personnel officers and the hotel's customers as well as other workers. Management was also not aware of the housekeepers' language needs with respect to their wider communication network in the hotel. The question of why the course was being offered required further discussion, exploration and, finally, agreement by both sides.

Interactions within these networks became subject matter for the course only after the co-ordinator helped managers expand their view of communication in the workplace. This means that, even in our initial meeting with sponsors, we should be prepared to help them view their perceived communication need in the context of a large network. Once the sponsor has accepted this more comprehensive view of a communication problem, we can then make a solid case for adequate pre-course development work in the form of a needs analysis.

In the first meeting with a sponsor, we are ideally negotiating for:

- Paid time for pre- and post-course development work.
- Access to the sponsor's human and material resources, such as supervisory and training personnel, documents, handbooks, etc., for information about the industry, the process and the product.
- Shared responsibility for determining the number and level of classes, as well as the makeup of each class.
- Shared responsibility for determining a suitable location, hours and support facilities.

PAYMENT FOR PRE- AND POST-COURSE DEVELOPMENT WORK

To ensure that appropriate objectives can be set for the course, the pre-course needs analysis should be presented as the essential first stage of a language and communication training program that provides the foundation for other aspects of the program. The results of the needs analysis, for example, feed into curriculum development and course delivery and the objectives established at this stage provide the basis for evaluating the effectiveness of the course.

In practice, the stages of the program, including the initial needs analysis, are not isolated but interactive. Although the bulk of the needs analysis work is done before the actual teaching begins, we are always investigating new needs, incorporating them into the course and evaluating their results.

Once they have committed themselves, many sponsors are anxious to see the course begin right away. They may have already made promises to the prospective learners or obtained tentative approval from their superiors. "If classes don't begin next week, the course may not be offered at all!" they may tell us. If we are clear about the importance of a needs analysis, we can present a convincing argument for it.

During the pre-course needs analysis, we familiarize ourselves with the working environment so that we can locate the prospective learners and their jobs in the larger structure. We then focus on the specific communication needs expressed by the sponsor and the learners, exploring them in relation to the overall communication network in the workplace. If union and management share sponsorship of the course, then we need ample time to investigate the views of both organizations in this manner.

At the end of the course, we also need adequate evaluation time to analyse our original objectives and the effects of the course on the learners and on the sponsoring organization(s). The more the sponsors are involved in planning the course, the more interested they will be in its outcome. Was the time and money invested in planning and delivering the course used wisely? A thorough review of the objectives and results of the course forms the basis for improved needs analyses at other sites. It can also help determine the objectives of a follow-up course in the same workplace.

ACCESS TO HUMAN AND MATERIAL RESOURCES

To do pre- and post-course development work adequately, we need access to the human and material resources of the sponsoring organization(s); that is, to all levels of personnel and as many relevant documents and audio-visual materials as possible.

CHANNELS OF COMMUNICATION

Early in the negotiations, we should become familiar with the channels of communication within the organization so that we can inform the appropriate people of what we will undertake in the various phases of the course. An organization chart with the names of personnel is one of the most useful pieces of documentation to request. In a larger industry or service organization, we might have to speak to supervisory staff at several different levels to ensure that each link person has been notified and consulted about the course.

> During negotiations with a large municipal department, one workplace teacher had arranged to meet the superintendent and the supervisor of a particular section. The supervisor was somewhat uncomfortable because his immediate superior—the superintendent—had not been contacted to discuss the program. The next day, the superintendent complained that someone in his department had been asked to co-operate in a program without his approval.

Obviously, in this instance, more thorough work during negotiations would have identified this superintendent as an important link in the chain of command. Whole courses can be jeopardized if the appropriate protocol is not followed by educators.

In a union-sponsored setting, it may be necessary to inform the regional executive as well as the local executive about the course, depending on the size of the union. Meetings of the education committee or the health and safety committee might also provide a good opportunity for teachers not only to become familiar with the issues but also to involve the committee members in the development of the course. Once again, it is important to follow the accepted chain of command. In one jointly sponsored program, for example, the union was largely responsible for advertising the course. The workplace co-ordinator and the teacher spoke with the local's vice-president, but unfortunately not with the shop stewards who would be receiving the notices for the course. As a result, very few of the shop stewards participated actively in the recruitment. The learners informed them of the details of the course rather than vice versa.

During negotiations with a large organization where learners may be drawn from a variety of departments, an efficient way to advertise the course and to introduce ourselves is to arrange for introductory group meetings with middle-level managers or union representatives—the people who are in daily contact with the prospective learners. This also clears the way to approach individual supervisors or shop stewards for detailed information later, once the learners have been selected.

ACCESS TO THE JOB SITE

To understand how specific communication needs relate to the wider communication network within an organization, it's a good idea to request access to the actual job site for at least part of one day. In a textile factory, for example, we would probably visit the floor and the various machines to observe the interactions. In a hotel or hospital, we might go through the routines with the housekeepers or service workers and note the types of activities and the range of linguistic and social skills demanded. One teacher who accompanied a hotel chamber maid as she carried out her morning duties commented on the unseen job pressures relating to the number of rooms to be cleaned in a specified period. This insider's view is one of the important results of a visit to the worksite. It helps explain the tension, fatigue and worries of workers, which often become part of class discussions.

Our observations can begin with a tour of the site but should not end there. Attending unit meetings, orientation sessions or special committees can also help us gain a more thorough understanding of the communication network within the working environment. Of course, access to job sites may be a sensitive issue if a manufacturer is worried about protecting industrial secrets, for instance.

Access to the actual job site also means that we have the opportunity to discuss communication needs with the specific individuals with whom the learners interact on a daily basis. This network usually goes well beyond the immediate supervisor or shop steward. It can include personnel staff, receptionists and secretaries, cafeteria staff, members of special committees and so on.

MATERIAL RESOURCES

In addition to the human resources that the sponsor has to offer, we should investigate the material resources available for use in the course. Management is usually more than willing to offer health and safety manuals, employee handbooks and company benefit forms. As the course proceeds, you may need to request more written materials, such as information on quality circles or employee involvement programs, job descriptions or performance assessment forms. Often the class participants can provide these documents as the issues come up for discussion. At the negotiation stage, it is important to ask about company or union policies that are likely to become the focus in class discussions of workplace issues.

For instance, in one corporate class, the company's own employee involvement program was reviewed and criticized after participants realized how differently various departments were managed. The promotion booklet describing the program and the expected outcomes was used as a model to analyse the management styles operating in each department.

SHARED RESPONSIBILITY FOR SELECTING LEARNERS

When sponsors have requested language training to address a particular problem, they will probably have pre-selected the learners. They may be people from one unit or department, as in the case of the hotel housekeepers who had to use new order forms. Or they may be people drawn from a variety of departments who will be involved in a specific task common to all of them. For instance, a union local may want to recruit more people for a shop steward course. Frequently, this apparently clear-cut view of needs becomes more complex as information about the course spreads throughout the workplace. In one hospital, for example, a course initially designed solely for the catering staff was subsequently opened to orderlies and dietary staff at their request.

During the early stage of negotiations, we can arrange for time to assess the language competence of the prospective learners, even if this assessment is informal. Formal oral interviews and brief reading and writing tests require at least one group meeting as well as private meetings for the oral interviews (see Chapter 4 for details about pre-course assessment of language skills). The final selection and placement of learners is accomplished best by examining the results of this assessment in conjunction with the needs analysis.

Management should also be warned about the negative effects of requiring employees to attend classes, especially when the class is held on the employees' own time. Employees who are forced to participate in a course may feel embarrassed at being singled out and resentful at being asked to give up their own time for training they didn't request. Or, they may feel that their job security is threatened—that performing well in the class is the only way they can keep their jobs. In cases like this, the teacher may have to spend many weeks in class trying to gain their confidence and trust. Rather than making attendance compulsory, employers might recommend attendance, explaining the long-term benefits and offering paid time or a bonus on successful completion of the course.

If the course is open to a wide range of people on a voluntary basis, publicity is a major factor in attracting learners. Who will advertise the course? How will they describe it? How will they promote it? Language and communication courses can be advertised incorrectly as "brush-up-your-grammar" courses. Sign-up sheets with introductory course information in English are unlikely to reach potential learners whose English is very limited. A written notice, even in the prospective learners' native language, may not be comprehensible to workers with a low level of literacy. If management or the union is responsible for recruitment and publicity, then our collaboration is necessary to ensure that accurate information gets to the appropriate people.

CLASS SIZE AND ATTENDANCE POLICIES

Class size is another variable open to negotiation. Under funding arrangements with some educational institutions, for example, an average attendance of 15 learners is required to initiate a course or provide an additional class in an existing course. Classes may start out with 15 or more, but often drop back to half this size because of layoffs, shiftwork, home responsibilities, inconvenient hours, etc. In cases like this, some workplace co-ordinators have negotiated for reduced student-teacher ratios and have successfully maintained classes with 10 learners or fewer. This smaller size is preferable because there will be a variety of educational backgrounds and individual problems no matter how homogeneous the class appears to be.

Because beginning literacy learners need a great deal of individual attention, class size is a particular issue when some or all of the learners need basic literacy training. Because classes are work-specific or even problem-specific, learners may view workplace courses as a one-time opportunity to take advantage of language training that is tailor-made for them. With these considerations and expectations in mind, classes usually function best with no more than 12 learners.

A few thoughts on attendance are worth mentioning. Because attendance can vary significantly and, at some stage, we will probably be reporting to the sponsor or the educational institution or both, we should be aware of the reasons for high and low attendance. Important factors are the overall economic environment, which could produce layoffs, and the specific conditions in the industry, such as production cycles, job rotation, shiftwork and so on.

We should also be aware of additional factors regarding attendance. If we are working with a funding formula from a government source, what are the benefits of that particular scheme to workplace classes? What are the drawbacks? In some cases, sponsors prefer to use attendance policies of their own, often those established for their staff training programs. For instance, the policy may state that if employees miss more than a certain number of classes within a certain period, they will be dropped from the rolls. Once again, what are the advantages and disadvantages of this for a language course? In other cases, the sponsor may ask the teacher to suggest a policy. For example, one teacher, approached independently by a multi-national corporation to set up a class for cleaners, was asked about an attendance policy. Management had already agreed to share the costs of the class, so a deal was being made between management and employees; each contributed half time. In cases like this, the details of a policy might best be left to management and the employees to decide. The teacher's suggestions may be most helpful if they are made on the basis of good classroom practice. For instance, if an employee must miss the first hour of every class, the teacher could help sort out the issue by asking if this is practical and beneficial from a teaching and learning point of view.

LENGTH OF COURSE

Courses lasting from nine to 12 weeks are most popular because they fit in with school board and college sessions and allow the sponsor(s) to review and evaluate frequently so that they stay in touch with the aims of the program. For courses of this length to be successful, we must be very adept at analysing needs and specifying objectives that are achievable within limited time periods. Sponsors are often more willing to commit themselves to short-term courses with limited objectives, a format they often use in their own staff development programs. It can also be easier to motivate learners in short spurts so that they can see and evaluate the results immediately.

It is important with short-term courses, however, to try to provide continuing classes so that learners can move through a series of levels. After 12 weeks, for example, basic level learners are often just beginning to feel comfortable with the classroom and the opportunity to continue learning should be provided. A series of short courses offers the possibility of regrouping, changing the location, rescheduling in relation to the workplace's busy and light seasons, and mounting special courses— for workers who have been laid off, for example. If classes can be integrated into company and union programs, short language courses can also provide bridges to other courses.

Because most workplace classes take place on company property, management must approve the location. Classes sponsored solely by a union, on the other hand, may be held in the union hall.

Clean, quiet and private rooms are ideal. These can often be found in hospitals, hotels, municipal departments, corporate offices and large-scale industrial workplaces. Boardrooms, staff training rooms and cafeterias have all housed workplace classes. However, in many small industries, such as textile factories, there is often only one space suitable for group meetings: the lunchroom or an area away from the machines. In these relatively open spaces, noise can be a problem if the factory is operating during class hours. And, even in unionized shops, teachers have reported that supervisory staff have taken advantage of these situations to observe the class, the content of the lessons and the remarks of the learners. Predictably, the learners become reticent, sensing that they are being watched, tested and kept in line by management's presence.

Because of a lack of privacy, one teacher felt that the only answer in her particular situation was to request that the next course be offered off the company property in a nearby community centre or school. In another case, the union took up the complaint, spoke to management and eased the tension so that a more supportive learning environment was restored.

At unionized and non-unionized worksites, teachers have found that inviting curious supervisors into the class is the best way of dispelling their fear and suspicion. Although learners may be reluctant to speak freely about their problems and complaints when a supervisor is present, gaining the confidence and trust of the sponsor serves the course better in the long term.

Selecting the hours for the classes depends on the availability of the learners, the shared-time or voluntary nature of the course and access to a suitable location. Classes tend to be most convenient when they are held at the end of the work day or shift. However, at this time, learners must battle fatigue and, in the case of many women, make special arrangements at home because they will be arriving late.

If learners are attending on their own time at the end of the work day, one- to two-hour classes are most common. A one-hour class three or four times a week provides frequent exposure to language in short, concentrated sessions and encourages a more conscious integration of language training into the daily work routine. On the other hand, a 1½- or two-hour class twice a week provides more time to explore issues and more possibilities for setting aside time to meet the specialized needs of individual learners.

Another alternative is a half-hour lunch-time session. Although this reduces the fatigue factor, it also has drawbacks. Half-hour classes do not provide enough time to explore the material in any depth. Furthermore, for workers, lunch is often a social time, their only real break from concentrated work. Nevertheless, when the learners are volunteers, their commitment to learn can help overcome these disadvantages.

In one textile plant, half-hour lunchtime classes were scheduled for each of the three shifts. Because learners were grouped according to shifts rather than language competence, the level of English proficiency in the classes was mixed and the intake was continuous. The boardroom location and good support facilities offset some of these drawbacks, but the commitment of the women and the teacher was the key factor in the success of this course. In another lunch program in the corporate sector, management set aside the boardroom for the two-hour class and also provided lunch as part of the 50-50 shared-time arrangement.

SUPPORT RESOURCES

The issue of who will supply support resources is also open to negotiation. Sponsors often provide access to copying facilities, blackboards, flip charts, secretarial assistance and refreshments, such as coffee, tea and juice. Storage space for materials is of great help and can often be arranged more easily than a chalkboard. Many teachers end up transporting their flip charts and materials from home to class and back home because have not inquired about the availability of storage space. Because these support resources are usually a matter of convenience, obtaining them can depend on establishing a good working relationship with the sponsor.

Because these negotiations are so important, teachers who are not directly involved in the process should be well-briefed on the procedures followed, the personnel involved and the results. Without direct involvement in the negotiations, teachers, as the deliverers of the course, may find it necessary to negotiate with educational institutions for paid pre- and post-course development work, for it is during these phases that good working relationships are developed and resource information obtained. More important, when teachers are involved throughout the entire process, communication between participants is recognized as a key factor in delivering and maintaining successful workplace programs.

CHAPTER 4 Conducting a Needs Analysis

S ue Folinsbee's chapter, "Conducting an Organizational Needs Assessment" (page 136), outlines the hows and whys of conducting a large-scale assessment that brings together key stakeholders in a partnership effort. The results and recommendations of this kind of organizational needs assessment (ONA) are often wide-ranging, covering many aspects of communications and employee relations.

The headings on the following page are from the table of contents of a completed large-scale ONA. In this investigation carried out by the organizers of a multicultural workplace program, it is clear that a variety of issues surfaced: organizational structure and policies; English-language difficulties; and conflicts involving issues of race, ethnicity and gender. The report identifies these problem areas and includes suggestions from employees for dealing with the issues, as well as detailed recommendations from the program co-ordinator.

Both *An Organizational Approach to Workplace Basic Skills: A Guidebook for Literacy Practitioners* by Sue Folinsbee (Waugh) and *Improving Intercultural Communications in the Workplace: An Approach to Needs Assessment* by Leslie Elver, Tara Goldstein, Joan McDonald and Julie Reid provide excellent guidance in developing investigative questions for large-scale needs assessments.

Although we highly endorse the comprehensive model, it is not always possible to investigate overall educational needs in this manner. The organization may resist an inquiry like this on the basis of the cost alone, or be unprepared to tackle the issues that will undoubtedly surface as a result of such a comprehensive assessment.

ORGANIZATIONAL NEEDS ASSESSMENT
TABLE OF CONTENTS

Adapted from material provided by Marni Johnson, Multicultural Workplace Program, Etobicoke Board of Education, Ontario.

Workplace co-ordinators report that it takes two to three months to complete the process—initiation, investigation, analysis and reporting—involved in large-scale organizational needs assessments. Because of this, they can realistically plan to conduct only three or four comprehensive assessments a year, unless they are able to pay teachers or consultants to take on this task.

In the absence of a comprehensive needs assessment, teachers are often required to gather their own information about the workplace and the needs of the learners. We refer to this kind of assessment as a small-scale needs analysis or program needs analysis. This chapter offers suggestions for conducting this kind of assessment, breaking it down into three stages: investigating and collecting data; analysing the data; and writing the report. Furthermore, it links the analysis of the data collected to the development of a workplace ESL curriculum.

INVESTIGATING AND COLLECTING DATA

Curriculums for workplace programs grow out of the learners' language needs in an employment situation. Because of this, the procedures and practices involved in developing and teaching a workplace course are radically different from those of most full- and part-time ESL programs, which usually focus on general language needs and fit the learners into a predetermined curriculum.

To determine the language and communication needs of a workplace, we must involve ourselves in the employment situation so that we come to know and "feel" the unique aspects of the workplace. The results of this investigation into the learners' communications needs are the basis for curriculum planning. Successful negotiations result in pre-course development time to investigate and collect data on learners' needs, to analyse those needs and to prepare course objectives based on the findings.

A needs analysis in the workplace usually involves three processes: interviews, observations and language assessment. These processes often overlap or take place concurrently. They are presented here as distinct steps only so that we can explore each thoroughly.

INTERVIEWS

Interviews with the prospective learners and a variety of personnel from the sponsoring organizations—the company or union or both—serve a dual purpose: they provide access both to information and to the people in the larger communication network. Through our investigations, we gather information about the structure and operation of the workplace, the learners' relationships and job responsibilities within this structure, and the language and communication requirements of the learners. We also have the opportunity to meet key people in the sponsoring organization(s). By clearly describing the aims of our course, we can win their support and enlist their assistance; in short, we can build the relationships that will ensure their co-operation and involvement. It is helpful to tape record the interviews with sponsors and learners, as long as they have agreed to this beforehand and do not feel awkward or uncomfortable about being recorded.

Interviews with Sponsors

To enable us to approach these key people in an efficient, professional manner, preliminary discussions with our contact person(s) provide us with some standard, basic information as follows:

- *Company details*: products; services provided; structure of the company; number of departments and employees; style of communication (oral or written); quality of working life, programs, and quality management; types of jobs; labour turnover; work schedules (shifts and layoffs); method of payment; benefits; promotion opportunities and requirements; health and safety instructions and records; orientation and other in-company training programs.
- *Union details*: structure of the union and affiliations; number of members and their level of participation at regular meetings; active committees; important clauses in the collective agreement relating to seniority, pension, health and safety, etc.; relations with management; method of communicating with members (especially non-English-speaking members); the election, duties and accessibility of shop stewards.

With our contact person(s), we also identify the specific people in the company or union to be interviewed, if this was not done during negotiations. In a large organization, it is best to start with senior personnel. Our purpose in meeting them is to make personal contact, describe the needs analysis and request that information be passed through the appropriate communication channels. If this communication works well, floor supervisors, middle managers and shop stewards will have been informed about us ahead of time and will be expecting to meet us.

Because senior administrators are responsible for approving the course, they are likely to have discussed it already with staff. Furthermore, they often have interesting information highlighting the long-term goals of the organization.

> In a discussion with the workplace teacher, one senior superintendent from a municipal department mentioned that in a few years the company was going to encounter real difficulties in recruiting supervisors in the janitorial department. Company policy was to promote from within the section, but there seemed to be very few qualified candidates among the janitors. He saw the workplace course as one step in upgrading their qualifications for promotion. In a subsequent meeting, shop stewards reiterated that 85 per cent of the janitors did not have the English-language skills necessary to obtain jobs that involved either lighter manual work or higher pay levels. In this instance, the same problem was defined from two different perspectives.

Our next interviews are with people who have direct, daily contact with the learners. From the company perspective, the interviews would be with the learners' immediate supervisors; from the union perspective, they would usually be with the shop stewards. This supposes, of course, that the learners have been at least tentatively identified.

It's important to be particularly observant and sensitive during these meetings, because staff at this level aren't usually consulted about the advisability of offering the course. For example, they may have been told that the company has decided to hold the course, but not why. They may receive some information about the course but they are often not told that they will be required to spend time talking to us or perhaps even release employees from work for interviews and assessments. If production is affected, supervisors may react negatively to the very idea of the course. They may respond by saying, "I don't know why they need a special program. Everybody else makes it on their own, don't they?"

Or, they may feel that the course somehow implies that they are being criticized by management. It isn't unusual for a supervisor to say, "I really don't see why my people need this course. The section runs smoothly. They're doing okay. After all, they don't need to read and write to do this job."

Or, in cases where the jobs involve an assembly line, supervisors may react negatively because they fear the classes will interfere with their ability to meet production quotas. Or, they may see no immediate use for language training. From their perspective, communication is not really part of the job, as indicated by this response: "For the work they do, they don't need to read English. They don't even need to speak English. It's bad enough when they talk to each other in their own language."

If we encounter negativity at this level, it's easy to predict the kinds of conflicts that may surface in the classroom. Negative comments from supervisors can be defused somewhat by focusing initially on *their* jobs, their responsibilities and their problems in dealing with a multilingual, multicultural workforce. Their comments, though sometimes difficult to respond to, are useful in "getting a feel" for the environment in which the learners work. Is there outright discrimination, or is prejudice expressed more indirectly through jokes and apparently harmless remarks? Will the environment be supportive for learning? If we ask ourselves questions like this, we will certainly be more sensitive during subsequent interviews and observations at the worksite.

Even supportive supervisors may find it difficult to be specific about communication problems because they have probably taken measures to compensate for poor communication over the years. Using interpreters, miming, or gesturing may be standard practice. Basically, they have accepted—through use—a level of communication with immigrant workers that they would never accept as adequate with native speakers.

Workplace educators suggest that interviewers ask "how" questions to enable supervisors or shop stewards to describe their communication systems—"How do you tell people about a new safety measure?" or "How do you complain about and remedy poor workmanship?"

Answering these questions can be revealing for the supervisors and shop stewards themselves. They may become more conscious of their frequent need for interpreters or of the inadequacy of the simple nod and "okay" they interpreted as understanding from workers who are unable to ask for clarification. General questions such as, "Can everyone follow instructions?" might result in an immediate "Yes." On the other hand, a more specific question, such as, "How do workers tell you when they don't understand instructions?" can help the supervisors analyse their own interactions with workers.

Some program organizers distribute written questionnaires to supervisors and shop stewards, especially in large organizations where learners are drawn from a variety of departments. If possible, teachers should take part in this activity so that respondents feel they are consciously part of our pre-course development process.

We can use the questionnaire to provide structure for a face-to-face interview or as a follow-up to a meeting with supervisors or shop stewards in which the aims of the program are discussed. If we invite supervisory staff to a modified focus group, they can fill in the forms collectively. Their involvement and awareness at this stage encourages them to feel at least partly responsible for the success of the course. An example of a questionnaire for supervisors follows on the next three pages. It's worth noting that the literacy skills of some supervisors may not be up to filling out this kind of questionnaire. When this is the case, it can be administered orally.

A sawmill successfully involved supervisory staff in a focus group to fill out an extensive questionnaire. The wide-ranging discussion that complemented the activity helped make various departments aware of each other's problems, promoted co-operation and built wider understanding and support for the program.

Diagrams of Communication Networks

In *English at Work: A Tool Kit for Teachers*, Deborah Barndt suggests that each learner be asked to make a communication network diagram showing all the people she or he communicates with on the job. This activity encourages learners not only to contribute data for the needs analysis but also to begin to research their own communication patterns. It usually works well as an introduction to workplace communication in the first or second class meeting.

A network diagram that illustrates Pui Kwan's communications in her job busing at a hotel (see Chapter 2) is shown on page 43.

The three most important channels of communication are circled: restaurant manager and assistant manager, guests, and personnel manager. In conversations with her fellow workers, Pui Kwan almost always speaks Chinese. Her communications with managers and guests are always in English, but for different reasons and under different circumstances. Communications with the restaurant manager are task-related, involving the assignment of her station for the day and special chores, such as running for linens, making coffee and replenishing the buffet table. Her communication with the guests, however, is of a much more social nature. At the non-verbal

SUPERVISORS' QUESTIONNAIRE

Please complete this questionnaire about the employees you supervise.

Job title or titles

_____

_____

1. What are the duties of the job/jobs?

   _____

   _____

   _____

2. What are the steps required to perform the tasks?

   _____

   _____

   _____

   _____

3. What tools, machines or supplies are used in performing the task?

   _____

   _____

   _____

4. What skills and knowledge are required for this job?
   Examples—Reading information, calculating, filling in forms or reports, etc.

   _____

   _____

   _____

5. What health and safety factors are involved in performing the tasks?

   _____

   _____

6. How do employees report illness? To whom?

   _____

   _____

7. Does a lack of oral or written English skills hinder advancement for employees?

   _____

8. Does a lack of numeracy skills hinder advancement for employees?

   _____

9. Does a lack of technical training hinder advancement for employees?

   _____

10. Is there a need for some of the employees to upgrade their English or mathematics skills? How many?

   _____

11. Please list any specialized terminology used in this workplace.

   _____
   _____
   _____
   _____
   _____

12. Please provide a list of sample questions you might ask or instructions you might give during the day.
   Examples—
   Manufacturing: How many skids did you pack?
   Hotels: Which rooms need cleaning?
   Office: Where is the report from Friday's meeting?

   _____
   _____
   _____

13. What information would you like employees to give you during the day?

   _____
   _____
   _____

14. What are some of the questions employees ask you?

   _____
   _____
   _____

15. Do any of the employees...
   ...appear to understand English but carry out instructions incorrectly?
   Yes ☐ No ☐
   ...say "yes" when you give them an instruction, then check with others in their own language before carrying out the task?
   Yes ☐ No ☐
   ...seem to understand some things and not others?
   Yes ☐ No ☐
   ...have difficulty making themselves understood?
   Yes ☐ No ☐
   ...fail to phone in when late or sick?
   Yes ☐ No ☐
   ...fail to ask permission to do something?
   Yes ☐ No ☐

...fail to report accidents or safety hazards?

Yes ☐ No ☐

...sound quite aggressive in non-routine or stressful situations?

Yes ☐ No ☐

16. Please check the language elements you would like the employees to learn.

Understanding instructions ☐

Explaining problems ☐

Reporting and explaining machine or equipment breakdowns ☐

Job-related words ☐

General health and safety information ☐

Understanding WHMIS ☐

Dealing with the unexpected (give examples) ☐

_____

_____

_____

_____

Recognizing codes, labels, names, packages on the job ☐

Report writing ☐

Memo writing ☐

Charting information ☐

Social language ☐

Understanding benefits ☐

Understanding company policies and procedures ☐

Other

_____

_____

_____

_____

_____

17. Is there any other information you would like to give us?

_____

_____

_____

_____

_____

Supervisor's Name _____

Department _____

Company _____

Adapted from material provided by Marni Johnson, Multicultural Workplace Program, Etobicoke Board of Education, Ontario.

level, there are smiles and acknowledgments and, at the verbal level, small talk, enquiries about food and requests for directions. With the personnel manager, communication is usually job-related—enquiries about paycheques, vacation and benefits. Communications of a more personal or counselling nature may result from these enquiries if Pui Kwan's family life or home environment affect her job performance. This kind of diagram helps us become more conscious of the range and style of language required of the learners in our classes.

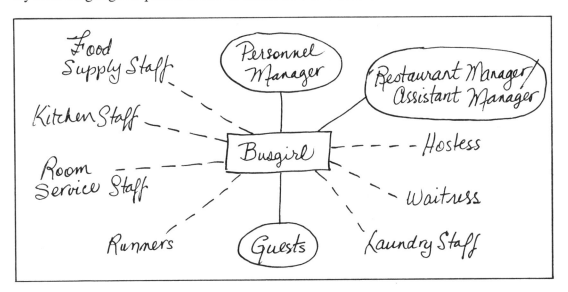

The teacher in Pui Kwan's hotel course also used the communication network diagram as a guide for determining whom to interview. The personnel manager, her company contact, produced the diagram with some basic information about the content of each of the communications. During the needs analysis, the teacher interviewed the restaurant manager, hosts, waiters, runners in the stewards' department and the laundry staff. She herself ate in the restaurant several times so that she could observe the interactions between the busing staff and the customers. On the basis of these interviews, she chose the three lines of communication already mentioned as the most important in terms of frequency of interaction, variety of tone and diversity of content.

In the diagram, we sketch out the lines of communication and assign priority to certain ones. Later, when we analyse the data, we will detail the types of communication that take place as the basis for curriculum planning. The people we interview can supply some of those details from their own experiences in communicating with the learners. Social language forms a considerable part of the communication in most jobs. Is contact with the learners social as well as work-related? How much socializing are learners currently capable of and how much is expected of them? Interviews with their coworkers who are native speakers might provide some useful information in this area.

At the basic level, the language learned could be as simple as greetings and complimentary statements. At more advanced levels, socializing might involve following up on an individual's particular interests, instructing a coworker in a task such as knitting, cooking or home repair, or perhaps understanding "in jokes" within the company or union.

Our interviews help us fill in the learners' communication picture and provide direction and material for class. Equally important, however, they help us build relationships at all levels within the sponsoring organization, encouraging input and participation in this first phase of the course.

In a textile factory, for instance, the receptionist can be asked about the procedure for calling in sick. We can tape a few of her calls so that we have listening materials for class. (Be sure to obtain the consent of both parties before using the tape.) In addition, we have gained an ally in the course. Having contributed to the planning, she will certainly be interested in its outcome and evaluation.

Printed and Audio-Visual Materials

During interviews with management and union staff, it's a good idea to inquire about printed documents and audio-visual materials produced by the sponsor that may be useful in the classroom. Materials that are commonly available from management are maps of the physical layout of the site, advertising brochures, employee handbooks with a history of the company and its regulations, benefit plans, safety manuals, training manuals, fire regulations, applications, payroll slips, employee newsletters or newspapers, and job descriptions or descriptions of routines that identify equipment used on the job.

Printed material specific to individual jobs varies with the worksite and should be requested in each interview. A waiter, for instance, may be required to read daily specials in addition to the regular menu. She may need to record notes in a log book as well as write customers' orders. In some restaurants, ordering has been computerized and waiters must learn the codes for items and how to key them in. People working in the corporate sector, especially finance, must routinely deal with forms, data, memos, and policy and procedure manuals.

Union representatives may also be able to supply some of these materials, as well as collective agreements, health and safety manuals, regular bulletins, newsletters or newspapers, and brochures on specific topics such as seniority, pension, work schedules, etc. Note that permission is needed to use the collective agreement in class.

In addition, large companies and unions often have films or slide shows for orientation purposes and staff development or in-service training. Of course, not all these printed and AV materials are useful in the classroom, but they can supply us with information about the sponsor, the requirements (from the sponsor's point of view) for effective performance and, in the case of management, the relationships between authority and the workers. They usually make fairly interesting reading and viewing for newcomers to a workplace, such as ourselves.

Interviews with Learners

In our pre-course interviews with the prospective learners, we can obtain necessary background information as well as their perceptions of their language and communication needs. Ideally, the purpose of these interviews is not to assess their language proficiency but rather to collect data to determine course objectives. Unfortunately, because of the limited time and resources available in many programs, these initial interviews focusing on personal information and educational background often end up serving as the language assessment.

Learners may be asked to fill in a short form with their name, address, ESL training, job title, etc.—all of it necessary information, but inadequate for determining language competence. If learners help each other fill in these forms, as they often do, the results can lead to major misconceptions about an individual's competence in English. Recalling Satvant's profile in Chapter 2, we can see how the teacher was misguided about her apparently strong reading skills. In fact, Satvant compensated for her poor reading skills by seeking help from coworkers as she had always done.

Furthermore, the questions on these forms are often familiar to most immigrants. Though they may be quite capable of filling in these forms themselves or of answering similar questions orally, this may not necessarily be a reliable indication of their level of competence and understanding in an interactive situation. In cases where learners' speaking and listening skills in English are low or when they are hesitant about using English, it is best to conduct the interview in their native language if possible.

Interviews with potential learners provide rich sources for determining course objectives as well as important opportunities for raising their awareness of themselves as learners. If they have thought about their language and communication needs before the course begins, they can make a communication network diagram in the first or second meeting. Armed with these descriptions of their own communication patterns, they will be better able to set reasonable goals for themselves, evaluate their progress throughout the course and continue learning after the course. If the learners are beyond the basic level, it's a good idea to find out to whom they speak English now. To whom would they like to speak English? Do they express the most concern about oral or written language?

For basic learners, general questions such as, "What do you want to learn?" can serve as an ice-breaker but don't usually produce any concrete information. The answer may be "everything" or "more words." We can focus on the tasks they perform in English by asking more specific questions, such as:

- "Do you speak English to your supervisor? About what?"
- "Do you call when you are sick? What do you say?"
- "What do you do if your machine breaks down? Who do you talk to? What do you say?"
- "Who did you speak to in English today? About what?"

At more advanced levels, learners may be able to specify the reading and writing tasks they are required to perform on the job. With our assistance, they may be able to assess their competence and begin to think about their goals. Is English needed for promotion or training within the company or for committee work with the union?

Some of the information we request in these interviews may require the learners to be willing to trust us. Although learners are frequently more open with teachers than with supervisors, it is important that we begin by introducing ourselves and explaining why we are holding the interview. Whatever help they can give us will make the course more useful for them.

Questionnaires designed to gather both background information and specific language information are often used in interviews with learners. This one-on-one setting allows teachers to explore issues sensitively, being aware of literacy problems and the need for interpreters for detailed explanations. The first of the two questionnaires that follow asks the learner to provide information about using language at home and in the community as well as at work. Language courses in many workplaces are not simply job-specific but are intended to address communication problems in the learners' personal lives as well.

In some situations, learners are familiar and comfortable with data-gathering procedures and can operate successfully on their own. The second questionnaire that follows (pages 49-50) is an information form that was developed for a business writing and grammar course in the corporate sector. The first part of the form includes standard background information questions used in all workplace courses offered by this board of education. The second part deals specifically with written communication at work, and requests samples of written work.

Learners can also supply printed materials or information for the course. They can bring to the first class handbooks, manuals, agreements, etc. that the company or union has given them. Simply finding the material at home and noting what they have received yet never read raises their awareness of their needs as learners. Armando, the municipal worker described in Chapter 2, realized that some of the reading tasks in class were based on safety books he had at home. His supervisor had given him the books when he started in the department but Armando had never really looked at them. He left class that night eager to find out what else he had at home that could serve his new interest in reading.

OBSERVATION

The second component of the investigation and data-collection stage is observation in the workplace, first involving a general tour of the entire site and then more specific observations in the areas where the learners work.

A tour of the worksite provides an overview of the entire process or service so that we can locate the learners' jobs in the whole. A tour of a hotel or hospital helps us understand how the job of housekeepers, for example, depends on the work done by a variety of other departments. Conversely, it also tells us which departments depend on the work of the housekeepers. A tour should give us a good sense of the physical

COMMUNICATION NEEDS

Name _____

Home Address _____

Home Phone _____

Job Title _____

HOME LIFE AND COMMUNITY LIFE

1. What is your first language?

   _____

2. What language do you speak at home?

   _____

3. To whom do you speak in your first language at home and in your neighbourhood?

   _____

   _____

   _____

   _____

4. Do you have difficulty using English in certain situations at home and in your community? Give some examples.

   Speaking

   _____

   _____

   Listening

   _____

   _____

   Reading

   _____

   _____

   Writing

   _____

   _____

5. Do you want to work on these difficult situations in class?

   _____

1. How long have you worked here?

_____

2. What is your current job?

_____

3. Have you done other jobs here? If yes, which ones?

_____

_____

4. Are there other jobs that you would like to do here? If yes, please name them.

_____

5. What languages do you use in your job?
   For speaking?

_____

   For reading and writing?

_____

6. Check the English skills that are most important in your job.
   Reading ☐   Writing ☐   Listening ☐   Speaking ☐

7. Do you have difficulty using English at work? Name the specific tasks that you find difficult.

   Speaking

_____

_____

   Listening

_____

_____

   Reading

_____

_____

   Writing

_____

_____

8. Would you like to work on these difficulties in class?

_____

PARTICIPANT INFORMATION FORM

Please complete the following questions. The information will help us design a course to meet your needs.

Date _____

Family Name _____   First Name _____

Current Position _____

Business Telephone _____   Department _____

Supervisor's Name _____

Date of employment with this company—

Month _____   Year _____

1. What languages do you speak?

   _____

2. What languages do you write?

   _____

3. How long have you been in Canada?

   _____

4. Have you participated in other English classes at work or outside of work?
   Yes ☐ No ☐
   If yes, where?

   _____

   How long?

   _____

5. Briefly describe your other education or training.

   _____

6. Describe your main job responsibilities.

   _____
   _____
   _____

7. Who do you need to write to at work?

   _____
   _____
   _____

8. Which of the following do you need to write and read at work? Please check.

	Never	Sometimes	Often
Telephone messages			
Memos			
Forms			
Instructions			
Letters			
Minutes of meetings			
Reports			
Work orders			
Evaluations			
Proposals			
Other (please specify)			

9. Which aspects of writing do you have difficulty with? Please check.

	Never	Sometimes	Often
Grammar			
Verb tenses			
Vocabulary			
Spelling			
Punctuation			
Organization/coherence			
Clarity/style			

10. What are the three most important things you would like to achieve or improve during this course?

_____

_____

11. What other reasons do you have for taking the course?

_____

12. Please attach three recent, *unedited* samples of your writing (e.g., a memo and a letter as well as a few paragraphs describing your expectations of the course).

Adapted from material provided by Kristine Copkov and Florence Guy, Multicultural Workplace Program, Continuing Education, Board of Education for the City of Toronto, Ontario.

layout of the workplace, especially if we have obtained a map beforehand. Where are facilities such as lunchrooms, washrooms and aid stations in relation to the learners' actual worksites?

Like the interviews, the tours also function as opportunities for advertising the course and meeting the wide variety of people involved in the successful operation of any company. In a program jointly sponsored by management and a union, a tour of the union local office is the best way to meet the staff—the committee members and secretaries—who could provide suggestions and assistance during the course.

More specific on-site observations can take a half day to several days to complete, depending on the size of the sponsoring organization(s), the diversity of learners' jobs, the variety within those jobs and the number of people in the learners' communications network. Through these observations, we hope to gain a perspective somewhat closer to the "insider's" view. We are interested in the unseen demands of the work itself, which may cause fatigue, frustration and complaints.

> In preparation for one course, the teacher worked in a hotel restaurant during the morning shift. She finished her shift with a new understanding of the interdependence of all the jobs and of some of the demands and pressures everyone faced.

> In a textile factory, a teacher went through the entire process of making a garment herself. She used all the machines under the instruction of the supervisor and her future students. Besides gaining the insight that comes from doing a job and living through its frustrations, both these teachers certainly achieved a new visibility and respect among management and among their future students.

Unfortunately, not all educational institutions or sponsoring organizations are willing to approve this type of participation. More commonly, teachers can accompany some of their learners through their daily routines as in a hospital or hotel setting. Or we can follow learners through the various procedures and tasks in an industrial or corporate setting. When the procedures are complicated or the names of the equipment and materials are unfamiliar, it's helpful if a supervisor, shop steward or the company or union contact person is available to explain.

Our observations can also help us fill in the specifics of the communication network diagrams. We should look for the occurrence of social language—when, where and with whom—in our diagram. What language is used when performing certain tasks and procedures? Where are the gaps between the language required and the language our learners can use? For instance, can they get help quickly if their computer is down? In a hotel or hospital setting, can they respond to a question like, "Where is the telephone?" In what circumstances are interpreters needed? How often does this happen, over what issues, and what procedures are followed? While these exact situations may not arise during our visit, there will certainly be opportunities to observe the learners' language competence in both initiating and responding in oral interactions. What written materials do they deal with on a daily basis? Is the ability to read and write important for carrying out their jobs? If they can deal adequately or even automatically with the printed material required for their jobs (e.g., time sheets, work tickets, routine forms, etc.), this can become the starting point for improving their reading and writing skills in class.

Observations can also give us a feel for the interaction dynamic of the workplace. First, we might take notice of the physical environment—the noise level, the physical distance between people, the number of opportunities for communication with fellow workers, and so on.

One teacher, scheduled to work in a course for hotel restaurant staff, spent a few hours "incognito" in the restaurant at tea time and lunchtime. The future students waited on her and responded to her requests in their normal manner. Besides monitoring language use and needs, she was also able to observe the tone of the verbal communications between native and non-native English speakers as well as the non-verbal cues, such as eye contact, gestures and facial expressions. She found, for instance, that one waiter always frowned and raised her eyes in frustration whenever she had to talk to the busing staff. She appeared impatient; her attitude was often demeaning. Cues like these are especially indicative of people's attitudes and the atmosphere in the working environment.

Another teacher working in the corporate sector listened in on the cross-country telephone calls students answered as part of their jobs. Although they generally handled these calls with ease, the teacher noticed that they had great difficulties in another area—participating in meetings. None of the learners was used to the interruptions, competition for talk-time and showmanship that characterized these office meetings. Predictably, the learners were silent or upstaged by colleagues or supervisors.

Virginia Sauvé has recommended that needs analyses incorporate anecdotal records "to demonstrate attitudes and specific relationships. If the atmosphere is tense, what seems to make it so? If, in the eyes of one person or group, you detect hostility, are there any clues as to why this is so? Who communicates with whom and under what circumstances? Who appears not to communicate with others?...These are some of the kinds of questions an observer should be asking."

Workplace Photos

In some programs, the tour is combined with a photo-taking session so that the photographs of work in progress can be used in the classroom later on. In a small industry, this technique works well, especially if most of the workers are familiar with the entire production process. In large industries, where learners may be drawn from a variety of departments, taking photos at this stage may be premature.

Of course, in some workplaces, photographing the equipment or process is not allowed for security or patent reasons or because of working conditions that might violate employment standards regulations. Regardless of the setting, it is important to get permission, oral or written, to photograph the site and the employees.

The use of the photos in class is often linked to describing job procedures and safety measures. The most useful photos are usually job-specific, capturing the learners in their own work routines.

Photos that document the chronology of a worker's day are also useful in class but depend on our knowing what door workers use to enter the building, where they go on arrival, where they spend coffee breaks and lunch hour, who they talk to throughout the day and how they get to and from work. This kind of information is more easily obtained through specific on-site observation or from the learners themselves rather than from a general tour. For this reason, some teachers prefer to wait until classes begin to take photos or to make the learners responsible for photographing their own workplace. Other teachers have suggested that the sponsor take the photographs and either mount them or prepare a slide show as a contribution to the course materials. Photographs can also be taken of the different signs that people have to read at the workplace. These are particularly useful in working with learners whose literacy skills are at a basic level.

LANGUAGE ASSESSMENT

We assess workers' language competence in a workplace setting to place learners, to diagnose language problems and to evaluate progress. At the program needs analysis stage, we are primarily interested in grouping learners, although tasks designed with the identified language needs in mind would also be useful in diagnosing weaknesses in certain skills.

Overall language competence and particular skills can be assessed in a variety of ways, ranging from an informal talk to formal testing. In this section, we will give examples of assessments that can be used as alternatives to formal testing.

Why Alternatives?

When we refer to formal tests, we include standardized generic tests as well as tests that have been custom-made for workers at specific sites. At the needs analysis stage, language tests are often used to select people who need training. The testing may be carried out within a particular department or across the entire workforce.

At a second stage of needs analysis, language tests can be used with the group chosen for training both before and after the course. This method uses a pre-determined set of test items that are usually work-related. In the pre-test, learners' skill levels are determined by seeing how well they do at certain communication tasks. In the post-test, their progress is assessed by checking how well they complete the same tasks.

While this methodology may seem sound, it's worth knowing that formal tests in a workplace setting are compromised by enough factors that we feel it is best to use alternative methods whenever possible.

First, consider the place of formal tests in a workplace culture. How many organizations or human resources departments use testing to decide a worker's suitability for other types of training? Is testing part of the workplace environment— are tests used to select candidates for promotions, transfers, further training, etc.? In many cases, organizations make decisions about promotions and training based not on the results of formal tests but on performance, contributions to the company, seniority or other experience-based criteria. Employees are constantly assessed in informal ways, just as we routinely assess the learners' progress through the communication activities we design ourselves.

Many organizations have introduced performance reviews and self-assessments that are much broader than a formal test. In addition to assessing performance, these reviews take into account overall goals, organizational style, issues and problems. They also offer some opportunity for dialogue, even though power is not evenly divided.

When traditional, formal tests are introduced into settings where they are not part of the normal routine, participants often voice the following concerns:

- Why do I have to take this test?
- Why isn't everyone taking it?
- Who decides if I pass or fail?
- Do I get to see my test results?
- Who else finds out about the test results?
- What will happen to my job?

It is very difficult for teachers to offset these negative views of testing. Often, attempts at thorough, clear communication do not reach the people we are most concerned about. Practices, attitudes and atmosphere in a workplace may run counter to our assurances about confidentiality, trust and job security. Access to test results is a matter of great concern to workers, particularly in programs where their progress statistics become part of their work records or data used to decide whether the workplace courses will continue. Employees may be justifiably fearful that management will use the test results as a cause for demotion or dismissal. Mandatory, rather than voluntary, testing can make employees feel resentful, singled-out or negative about participating in a course.

In addition to the issues of appropriate use, attitude and confidentiality, other problems with formal testing also need to be considered. Crowded conditions during testing make it easy for learners to consult each other about the written test, thus reducing its validity. Tests designed for a specific group of learners (e.g., those with more oral than written fluency) may not be challenging enough or suitable for another group of learners.

Examples of Alternatives to Testing

To explore alternatives to formal testing, we'll examine two examples: one is a large hospital introducing new technology; the second is a small organization with varied language needs that is bringing in new, expert technical staff.

> Like many other large-scale health centres across the country, the hospital decides to revamp its food services department to achieve greater efficiency, expanded choice, improved service and—potentially—more profit. With a new computerized menu program, administrators believe that the hospital might be able to take on private contracts, such as Meals on Wheels, and turn a profit in the future. Managers know that a significant number of dietary staff will not be able to use the system without literacy and higher basic skills training.
>
> How will they find out who needs training—and who will pay for this kind of assessment? The workplace co-ordinator and the hospital decide to require everyone, including the supervisors in the department, to take a written test (custom-made for the hospital) so that basic skills can be addressed before computer training begins. About 130 people must be tested and, although the co-ordinator prefers interview-style assessments, no one is willing to pay for the weeks of testing and analysis this would involve or to delay the course while this happens. The solution is to test people in groups of 15 over an eight-day period.
>
> Problems arise because workers are not used to formal testing and try to help each other during the test. Despite what the co-ordinator thought was a clear and thorough presentation on the purpose of and procedures involved in the test, some write nothing, saying they don't understand why they have to be tested at all.
>
> Employees express confusion, fear and anger. While the co-ordinator and instructor are not pleased with the process, they see no other way of meeting the hospital's need for quick action. In the end, 40 people are identified for the training course and the co-ordinator insists that it be conducted completely on company time.

Unfortunately, organizations frequently call workplace educators when they are already in crisis and want problems resolved immediately with the least possible disruption in their routine. But, as we know, education doesn't happen this way. A successful workplace education program depends on all the stakeholders giving their time, patience, commitment, trust and willingness to meet the challenge of change. The change involved here is not technological change, but the change that takes place in people as they grapple with new ideas, new skills and a new sense of themselves.

Let's examine what might have happened if this situation had been approached differently. The technology is in place but some of the workers are not ready to use it. To maintain their jobs, they know that they must learn new skills. In these circumstances, an advisory committee would seem essential for success. Representatives from management, the union, the human resources department and the dietary staff, as well as the workplace education provider and perhaps other stakeholders (board, patients, relevant hospital committees) would be key members of the committee. They need to discuss the impact of this technology and form a focal unit providing support, communication and guidance in integrating the new technology. This advisory committee could begin by:

- Providing information and hands-on demonstrations of the computer system.
- Reviewing the manuals and instructions to see that they are comprehensible. If not, they may need to be illustrated and rewritten in plain language.
- Assessing the computer training that will be offered. What educational level is needed to complete the training successfully? Can the training be modified to achieve acceptable results at a less advanced level?
- Providing information sessions to small groups of workers about the new system and its impact on their jobs, as well as plans for basic skills education to prepare for further training.
- Scheduling private and confidential "consultation time" for workers to discuss education and training with the instructor.
- Advertising basic skills courses and providing encouragement and support for workers to enrol voluntarily.

If the basic skills program for those who don't pass the test is voluntary rather than obligatory, then we have taken one step towards willing participation. Of course, in situations like this, employees realize that they must upgrade or face the real possibility of losing their jobs.

As educators, we know that a supportive educational environment encourages exploration, reduces fear and helps people meet a challenge with greater prospects of achieving success. If employees feel reticent about discussing their need in small group information meetings, then private consultation time with an instructor might allay their fears and offer the personal assistance needed to overcome hesitation. Spending time doing this kind of preparatory work, rather than testing, would reap more rewards: more positive employee relations; willing participation of the workers in a course; and a partnership spirit in the organization.

Despite everyone's best efforts, there will probably be a small number of employees who need basic skills training but do not volunteer for the courses. In these cases, union or management might encourage them to sign up for a consultation session to talk about the skills needed for using the computer system. These sessions are not "private tests," but a time to discuss difficult issues confidentially. The discussions might include their past experiences with and attitudes toward education, an informal analysis of the communication skills needed to perform their current jobs, and their own assessment of their skills. In these sessions, employees may reveal personal issues and company difficulties that affect their participation in education; therefore, absolute confidentiality must be ensured.

If this effort fails, these employees will have to tackle the computer training without preliminary upgrading. Perhaps they will succeed; if not, they will have no choice but to enrol in the program to maintain their jobs.

A small organization hires specially trained technical staff to work with a new system. They speak English as a second language, as do some of their department colleagues who have more seniority in the company. Maintenance and cleaning staff are predominantly immigrants from a variety of educational backgrounds who need ESL training. The company wants to make the best use of its new technical staff and asks for assistance in setting up an ESL program.

After a small-scale needs analysis, one of the educational services proposed is an ESL workplace class. Because there are speakers of English as a second language working throughout the company, the invitation to join the class is issued company-wide. Attendance is voluntary. The class draws 12 people from four different departments whose oral and written skills range from basic to advanced.

In order to group learners, it is necessary to find out their level of skill in listening, speaking, reading and writing. While the speaking and listening skills of some may be adequate to perform their jobs and survive in the wider community, their reading and writing skills may be very weak. Even when their skills are weak, there may be some areas, such as personal information and job-related vocabulary, over which they have good control. Other learners may be at the absolute beginning stage in all four skills and may even need pre-literacy training if they do not have much experience with the printed word.

With such a wide spread of skills among so few people, do we test on the first day of class? Some workplace teachers have expressed reticence about placement testing because they believe it is too intimidating for the learners, especially for those who have volunteered to attend classes. This can be particularly true for learners whose formal education is many years in the past or whose previous language learning experiences have not been satisfying.

We can begin with this mixed group by suggesting that they think about what they need and what they want to accomplish; in other words, invite them to conduct a personal needs assessment. A questionnaire, such as one of those described earlier in this chapter, can be filled out by the intermediate and advanced participants, while the basic level learners can be interviewed individually or in a small group with the instructor filling in the questionnaire when necessary. If their oral skills are good enough, they can talk about their jobs and their language needs at work and at home. We can ask them to:

- Describe their job or one of the processes involved in their job.
- Give short instructions on how to perform one part of their job.
- Describe what they do if they're sick and can't go to work.
- Describe what they would if their supervisor asked them to work overtime and they couldn't.
- Describe what they'd do if their paycheque were wrong.

If this is too demanding, then try using pictures that are work-related so they can talk about what they do.

Another method that has worked successfully is to talk to learners who are at a basic level in all four skills in groups of three or four. Each introduces him or herself and exchanges personal information—with the help of bilingual teachers or interpreters, if necessary. Learners can also be asked to write their names on cards and, after more informal talk, they can try to write their addresses or the name of the country they come from. Can they write this without help from somebody else or without referring to an envelope or piece of paper they carry with them? In this way, some information about their oral and written skills can be obtained although, as mentioned earlier, we should be aware of the problems that may result from using this informal method of deciding placement.

Other procedures that can be carried out in the first few days of class to help diagnose literacy problems are described in *A Handbook for ESL Literacy* by Jill Bell and Barbara Burnaby. In addition, individual discussions with the intermediate and advanced learners about their responses give us some idea of how well they can talk about themselves, their jobs and their needs. In this way, everyone in the class begins to analyse their own needs, an important step in setting objectives for the course.

These informal interactions with the participants will provide enough information to group learners at different levels initially. In a group with a variety of skills and jobs, different groupings for oral, reading and writing tasks may be necessary. *Teaching Multilevel Classes in ESL* by Jill Bell contains some excellent suggestions for organizing this kind of class.

ANALYSING THE DATA

Analysing the data we have collected entails identifying the common concerns about communication that arose during our investigations and relating them to the results of the language assessment. This may involve dealing with questions such as:

- What problems are repeatedly mentioned by both learners and sponsors in our interviews?
- On what issues are there conflicting information or a mismatch of opinions?
- What common language requirements are referred to?　　.
- Do our own observations in the workplace confirm these commonly stated concerns?
- Do the learners and sponsoring organizations express similar needs? If not, it may be best to find the areas of overlap rather than consider the two points of view to be mutually exclusive.

Information from our interviews with management, the union, learners and their coworkers, as well as the assessment data, indicates where the learners can and cannot cope with the language demands of their workplace and perhaps of their wider community.

A workplace program in a municipal service commission drew skilled and semi-skilled workers from several departments. In the interviews, the most commonly stated concerns involved reading and writing skills.

Managers felt that the workers should be able to read safety manuals and important memos relating to job performance. In an effort to maintain the high safety standards of the commission, they were proposing annual safety exams for all employees. Over the long term, they hoped that the workplace course would upgrade the reading skills of the semi-skilled, hourly-rated workers. Many of these workers had been commission employees for more than 10 years and might now find their jobs in jeopardy if they couldn't pass the safety exam. Only one supervisor gave listening and speaking skills top priority. He used the telephone almost exclusively for communicating with the workers.

Union representatives echoed the main concerns of management, but also felt that improved reading and writing skills were necessary for retraining workers to ensure job security. The workers themselves wanted to begin where they felt their skills were weakest—writing for the job and for personal use. Placement interviews partially confirmed their own assessment of themselves: writing was the weakest area, reading also needed improvement and oral interaction skills varied widely. Fortunately, the group divided naturally into two classes on the basis of skills and job location.

While both classes worked on reading and writing skills, Group A, operating out of a different location from Group B, placed equal emphasis on the oral interaction skills identified by their supervisor.

In this situation, a communication network diagram helps describe the workers overall language requirements in terms of communication tasks. It also provides a framework for asking questions and recording and categorizing information so that there is an interplay between investigation and analysis. What similar items were mentioned in different network channels? How many people mentioned the same communication task as a source of difficulty?

Because many communication tasks overlap and involve a variety of people, we are likely to hear the same problems repeated. For instance, reporting a machine breakdown in a sawmill can put the worker in contact with the mechanic, the supervisor and possibly the union representative if, for example, continued requests for assistance are not met. Understanding oral and written instructions might involve contact with the supervisor, the mechanic, the union health and safety representative and the personnel manager. Calling in sick usually requires communication with the receptionist and with the supervisor. Do several communicators comment on language or culture-related problems associated with one task? When a problem is reported through one channel of communication, do staff involved in other channels agree that it is a priority?

These examples illustrate the interplay between investigating and analysing. These two procedures also affect the process of curriculum planning. Continuing analysis while data are being collected helps us focus our questions and observations with a view to developing the curriculum. All three procedures serve the others and are structurally linked, though they are highlighted at different times throughout the development and planning of a course.

We begin with an emphasis on investigation informed by analysis and by our goal of planning an appropriate curriculum. During the concentrated analysis stage, we study the collected data carefully for the purpose of writing objectives. A curriculum with overall course objectives and more specific classroom objectives is not carved in stone, but is a working document. Its first form is based on the results of our needs analysis. With the variety of interests to be served in every workplace program, new interests and needs inevitably come to light as the course progresses. Investigation and analysis continue, always informing our choices and our reflections on the working curriculum. In addition, if we and the learners are evaluating the objectives regularly throughout the course, we need a curriculum that can be responsive. Do the original objectives remain relevant? Are they too broad? Too narrow? A keen awareness of the continuing and interactive role of investigation, analysis and evaluation with respect to curriculum planning helps to ensure that a responsive curriculum is developed.

As an example of the way these processes are interlinked, we'll look at data collected for a workplace program involving a group of housekeepers in a medium-sized hospital.

> The program was initiated by hospital management because supervisory staff noticed that the housekeepers displayed persistent difficulties in following instructions and reporting damages, and continued to need interpreters to deal with complex personnel and payroll problems, the course was sponsored jointly by the union and management. Union officials agreed to the course primarily because they saw a need for more health and safety education. At that time they were also in arbitration on an issue that could affect the housekeepers. The shop steward, a native speaker of English, felt that improved language skills would help the housekeepers stay abreast of the issue.

The communication network diagram that was produced is shown on the following page. As the diagram indicates, the lines of communication most frequently used were with the patients, fellow workers, the head housekeeper and the shop steward. Although socializing with the patients was not actually included in the housekeepers' job description, this interaction was the most frequent and often the most satisfying. Initiating comments by the housekeepers included enquiries about health, family and the daily TV soap opera, as well as words intended to cheer up and sympathize. In return, housekeepers might be asked about their families or jobs or expected to react to complaints ("My family never visits me."), requests ("Close the blinds." "Call the nurse."), and even insults ("You people are so rude. You never answer me.").

A good relationship with patients relies on an understanding of the importance that attitude, perception and emotions play in communication. In this particular hospital, the housekeeping staff represented a wide variety of ethnic groups, so socializing among fellow workers was usually in English. At coffee breaks and lunch, the topics of conversation included family concerns, health issues, entertainment (bingo), daily work-related matters, and current union issues.

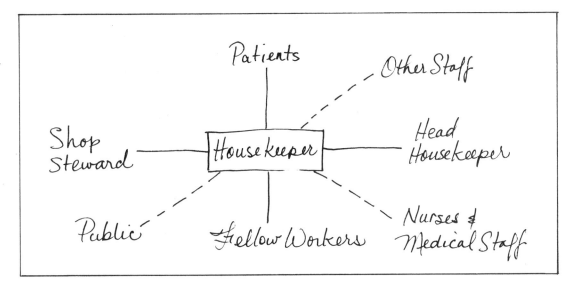

The housekeepers' relationship with the head housekeeper was such that communication between them was strictly business. There was little inclination on either side for informal conversation. Their communication focused on complaints about the quality of work, health and safety requirements, scheduling, ordering supplies, reporting damages and procedures such as phoning in sick, reporting accidents and requesting vacation time. So, although contact with the head housekeeper was not as frequent as with the patients and fellow workers, the information exchanged was essential to performing their jobs well.

Contact with the shop steward was especially frequent during the initial stages of this course because the workers were following a grievance filed on behalf of nutritional services workers that had been submitted to arbitration. The housekeepers were interested because the grievance involved layoffs that might affect their jobs.

Faced with a rather rigid hierarchy in the hospital, the housekeepers felt that they rated little respect from their superiors on the job. Their relationship with the nurses and other medical staff was observably cool. Nurses did not expect or invite communication with the housekeepers. The only real contact was that initiated by the nurses and usually involved job-related commands such as, "Do that room first." Once again, communication, although infrequent, was crucial for job performance.

Of the office personnel, only the payroll department had any significant contact with the housekeepers and this usually occurred when there were discrepancies in paycheques. Communicating with the general public—usually with visitors about directions to the cafeteria, etc.—was infrequent and not considered a priority.

During interviews and observations, the specific problems noted fell into four broad categories: job routines; personnel-related procedures; socializing and informal contacts; and communication in the wider community. These are outlined in the following list (the letters before each item indicate the source: S—supervisory staff, U—union, H—housekeepers).

Job Routines

- ■ S H   Following instructions or asking for clarification.
- ■ S U   Reading names of materials for ordering.
- ■ S U   Knowing health hazards associated with materials used.
- ■ S   Knowing names of furniture and items in rooms.
- ■ S   Knowing colours to identify coding for cleansers, etc.
- ■ S U   Understanding all the health and safety regulations.

Personnel-Related Procedures

- ■ S   Understanding the procedures for requesting vacation.
- ■ S H   Phoning in sick.
- ■ U   Being aware of issues affecting job category.
- ■ S U   Knowing procedures for filing accident reports.

Socializing and Informal Contacts

- ■ H   Feeling comfortable with some patients who want to talk.
- ■ H S   Responding to patients' enquiries, requests, insults.
- ■ H   Conversing easily with fellow workers on topics of common interest.

Wider Community

- ■ H   Filling out bank forms or writing cheques.
- ■ H   Writing phone messages or simple notes.
- ■ H   Making appointments with doctors, dentists.
- ■ H   Talking to children's teachers.
- ■ H   Understanding written notes from school.

This information, along with resource materials supplied by the hospital and the union, provided ample content for curriculum planning. The language assessment pointed to a common need for work on basic reading and writing skills. Although the participants' initial reading and writing levels ranged from basic literacy to high basic, their oral interaction skills were more noticeably divided between basic and high intermediate.

As a result, two classes were recommended based on the learners' mastery of listening and speaking skills—the skills that were most dissimilar in initial assessments and mentioned frequently during the investigations. The basic class was designed to pursue priority content information in tasks emphasizing oral interaction and basic reading skills. The intermediate class was built around tasks that more fully integrated the four skills with slightly more emphasis on reading and writing.

WRITING THE REPORT

Both informal and in-depth needs analyses involve a continuing effort to collect and analyse data. Through interviews, observation and assessment, we can get information to help us develop relevant lessons and materials. Just as important, we can establish a presence in the workplace by building relationships within the organization and by finding our place in the communication network.

Once we've collected and analysed the data, we must put together our recommendations and report to the organization. In most cases, a written report describing the needs analysis process and recommendations is negotiated and included in the initial costs, though sometimes an organization is satisfied with an oral report presented to management, union and staff representatives. In either case, it is important to make the results of the needs analysis available to key stakeholders and course participants.

REPORTS FOR ORGANIZATIONAL NEEDS ASSESSMENTS

At the beginning of this chapter, we took a brief look at the table of contents of an organizational needs assessment report. In these large-scale needs assessments, a written report is presented to the advisory committee (or key representatives) who then make it available company-wide. The best way to present the report is at a committee meeting so members can be "walked through" the findings and recommendations and ask questions. This helps build support for educational programs in the workplace.

ONA reports should include the following:

- Acknowledgements of and thanks to the organization and those who participated in the ONA.
- Executive summary of key findings and recommendations.
- Background of the organization including a brief history, changes in the industry and reasons for assessing training needs at this time.
- A description of the methods and processes (questionnaires, interviews, focus groups, etc.) used to gather information, along with the number of participants, their positions and departments. Copies of all questionnaires and interview guidelines should be included in the appendixes.
- Findings and recommendations with statistics, issues, analysis and specific training recommendations organized by topic. Recommendations arise from the data collected and must be supported by a solid interpretation and analysis. Quotes from participants in the ONA are effective in focusing attention.
- Appendixes, including copies of all questionnaires and guidelines used to collect information, as well as statistics and data not presented in the body of the report, advertising flyers for the ONA and more information on the process and findings that are of secondary interest.

A small-scale needs analysis is narrower in scope and provides information related to a specific workplace course. In the process of our investigation, other needs, such as training for computers, post-secondary certificates, anti-racism education, and plain English instruction, may surface. Although they are not the primary focus, these issues need to be documented in a report or oral presentation. It might be useful to restate them in a final evaluation.

These reports often include course objectives, even if they are preliminary, and possibly a description of activities designed to meet these objectives. In some cases, companies request detailed outlines of weekly topics and activities. Requests like this can result in the course becoming too tightly structured so that there is no flexibility to include new topics or skills as the need arises. It's best to insist that any course outline be considered a *working* document that is subject to change.

Reports for small-scale needs analyses usually include:

- Background information, including the name of the company and union, the education provider and the course title and dates.
- A description of the methods and processes (questionnaires, interviews, focus groups, etc.) used to gather information, as well as the number of participants, their positions and departments. Copies of all questionnaires and interview guidelines should be included in the appendixes.
- Findings—with specific information on communication, issues to be covered during the course, goals of the course and possible activities. A detailed outline can be included if necessary.
- Other educational needs, including further training needs, that can be considered in the future.
- Appendixes, including copies of all questionnaires and guidelines used to collect information and other information of secondary interest.

CHAPTER 5 Designing a Workplace Syllabus

Because workplace teachers are curriculum designers, we determine the objectives for our courses: what must be achieved overall, as well as what must be accomplished from day to day as we work toward reaching our primary goals. We not only choose the content or subject matter of the course, which can include knowledge and skills relating to language, the workplace and the community, but we also decide how we're going to cover this subject matter. The methods we choose are evident in the materials and lessons plans we develop for the classroom. Furthermore, we evaluate our choices, not only at the end of the course but also as the process unfolds.

Setting objectives, choosing content, developing materials, deciding on methods and evaluating their effectiveness: curriculum design includes all these activities. As a result, we take a broad view of curriculum. The activities do not take place in lockstep fashion, with setting objectives followed by developing materials and then evaluating. Rather, each activity informs and is integrated with the other. When we write objectives, for example, we outline subject matter to be covered. When we evaluate, we review our objectives and, possibly, revise them and the subject matter in light of our findings.

INTRODUCTION TO CURRICULUM DESIGN

Traditionally, curriculum specialists and textbook writers have been largely responsible for setting the agenda with respect to curriculum. In second-language teaching, however, teachers and learners are currently assuming more responsibility for curriculum design. Together, we discuss and agree on the overall goals of the course and the individual goals of each learner. Learners often become at least partially responsible for contributing the materials we work with in class. And, along with the teachers, they are active in monitoring and evaluating the progress of the course.

Another player—the sponsor—is also very important in the process of designing curriculum for workplace programs, playing a role in setting objectives, providing content materials and evaluating the results.

Because of the number of players and the variety of communication needs involved in workplace programs, teachers usually find that a new curriculum evolves or is designed for each course. This situation is different from that found in most general adult ESL programs in which the objectives and subject matter are predetermined. Their objectives are often stated in functional terms (e.g., greeting, requesting, refusing) and listed with corresponding grammatical structures (e.g., past tense, possessive pronouns). Or, the organizing principle may be stated in terms of themes and topics (The Law and You, Consumer Services, Education, Getting Started on Your Own) so that it is content that decides which functional and grammatical subject matter will be covered. For classroom materials, teachers often use commercial textbooks geared to the general ESL program.

In a workplace program, on the other hand, all the players engage actively in curriculum design. They determine the objectives and subject matter most suitable for the specific group of learners, and work with materials that are often tailor-made for each course. Each workplace and each group of learners is unique. In workplace programs, we have the good fortune to be in a position where the uniqueness of each program is seen as a benefit and as the motivating force for curriculum design. We also have the benefit of working in an important, relevant and immediate context. Workplace programs are naturally content-based, which means that we are all engaged in developing knowledge about work and life as well as the skills to express ourselves.

In this chapter and the two that follow, we will examine three activities involved in curriculum design:

- Designing a syllabus (that is, writing course objectives).
- Developing classroom materials and planning lessons.
- Evaluating the process and the results.

Because these activities are interrelated, it is somewhat misleading to talk about each separately. Therefore, although each chapter focuses on one of the activities, it also refers to the others that necessarily complement it.

THE SYLLABUS

When we design a syllabus, we write course objectives. This involves selecting and organizing the content of a course, a process that is directly related to the needs analysis (see Chapter 4) that has already been largely completed.

The investigation of needs does not stop once the needs analysis is complete; rather, it is a continuing activity that teachers and learners engage in throughout the course. The needs and the desires of the participants become topics of negotiation in the classroom, and decisions about how they can be fulfilled are made jointly. For instance, if the sponsor of a program has very definite aims that can be realistically incorporated and achieved, then we will probably begin the course with some predetermined outcomes in mind. Then, as new objectives emerge during the course, we can integrate them with the original objectives.

As the preceding chapter on conducting a needs analysis indicated, the process of writing objectives is interactive: investigating and analysing needs leads to the development of a preliminary syllabus that is responsive to the results of continuing evaluation and reflection. It promotes the idea of the curriculum as a "working document" in which there is a constant interplay among analysing, setting objectives and evaluating.

A workplace syllabus is also dynamic in another more practical sense; it responds to and incorporates a learner's daily needs. The day that Anna's paycheque is incorrect, for example, is the day to begin working on the problem. It is often in dealing with specific problems like this that a change in behaviour, an increase in self-confidence and the learning of coping skills can be achieved. When we respond immediately, we acknowledge the ability of the learners to identify what is important to them and provide an opportunity for them to exercise some of their controlling interest in the course. Workplace teachers often act on the belief that their first obligation is to the learners. Responding to Anna's paycheque problem by making it a language-learning activity for the whole class is one expression of that belief.

WRITING OBJECTIVES

In many workplace programs, sponsors or educational institutions or both request that course objectives be either presented formally in a written report or agreed upon informally in discussion. Even if the sponsors do not make a specific request, it is important to show them the course objectives before classes begin. It makes sense for them to confirm and help in developing the objectives before we begin putting together further detailed drafts and classroom materials. Equally as important, the objectives of the course define their expectations for improvement in the learners' communication skills.

EXAMPLES OF WORKPLACE SYLLABUSES

As a result of a needs analysis conducted in the workplace, a variety of communication tasks will probably have been identified as important and needing improvement.

For example, we might look at the tasks identified by the hospital staff and housekeepers on page 62 in Chapter 4.

When preparing a syllabus, it is better to start with a general statement of objectives rather than a list of specific tasks. The objectives provide an overall framework that helps us identify the sequence and growth of learning. Specific tasks are then placed within this framework, providing the "how" of reaching the objectives. The chart on the following page, for example, illustrates the objectives of an intermediate language course in a manufacturing company. They are grouped under the headings "Job-Related Skills" and "Community-Related Skills."

The job-related objective, "Understand company benefits package," for example, may involve a number of tasks, such as the following, that show how we would achieve this objective.

- Discuss what employees already know.
- In small groups, write a list of these items.
- Make a list of what students want to find out or are unsure of.
- Read sections of material outlining benefits package to find specific information and develop a thorough understanding.
- Practise filling out benefit forms.
- Do problem-solving in other situations to see if or how benefits cover employees.

In an article in *TESL Talk*, Jill Bell described how she developed a curriculum for a Levi Strauss workplace project. She developed five sections that covered both social and work-related situations. She found that working on the language required for social interaction provides non-threatening situations for increasing self-confidence, incorporates most of the basic structural patterns of English and motivates learners by raising passive knowledge to the active level. After establishing this base, more specific job-related topics were covered.

The course was designed in five sections, to be taught sequentially. Each section broke down into a number of units that could be taught in one lesson, or covered in greater detail over a number of lessons with students whose skills were less well-developed.

Here are the five sections Bell used to organize the course:

- *Section 1* covered some of the basic ground rules of the language. It aimed to activate the passive knowledge many students already possessed, thus increasing their confidence in their ability to learn. It also familiarized the students with the learning techniques that would be demanded of them.
- *Section 2* concentrated on using everyday social conversation with peers. The content was determined by the needs identified in the needs analysis.
- *Section 3* provided the basic language necessary for the work to be performed correctly and efficiently and reinforced the social conventions covered in Section 2.

COURSE OBJECTIVES
INTERMEDIATE LEVEL

JOB-RELATED SKILLS

Students should be able to—

Communicate well enough to inform and understand coworkers and supervisors—i.e.,

- request permission.
- respond to questions.
- make general inquiries.

Understand company benefits package.

Complete insurance, medical application and questionnaire forms.

Understand company structure and methods of manufacturing.

Know names of machines and production sequences and how to describe problems related to the machinery production.

Write detailed job description of their own jobs and those of others in the same department.

Read and understand memos.

Display appropriate problem-solving skills related to teamwork.

Understand the company's mission statement, values and guiding principles.

Have a general understanding of North American cultural norms.

COMMUNITY-RELATED SKILLS

Students should be able to—

Communicate greetings, introductions, invitations (making, accepting, refusing), thanks and apologies.

Understand directions and read maps.

Use telephone to leave or take messages, complain of dissatisfaction with service, etc.

Understand and discuss media advertising.

Read newspaper, TV listings, the *Yellow Pages*, and understand how to find information there.

Read and understand transportation schedules, driver's manual and safety rules.

Communicate with teachers at local board of education.

Read first aid manual and understand hospital procedures.

Pronounce clearly numbers and letters of the alphabet.

Adapted from material provided by Marni Johnson, Multicultural Workplace Program, Etobicoke Board of Education, Ontario.

- *Section 4* concentrated on the use of language on the job, applying previously learned structures to the situation on the factory floor. It also provided orientation information on company policy in areas such as safety and sickness.
- *Section 5* dealt with the use of language in high-pressure situations, such as disagreements or discussions with superiors. Orientation information on quality requirements and the payroll system were also introduced.

The content of this particular syllabus included work and social dimensions and was consciously designed to help learners progress from the known and familiar to the more challenging.

In a very different workplace setting, a financial institution requested a course outline as part of the program needs analysis report. The course had a single skill focus—oral proficiency—and the activities listed on the outline shown on the following page demonstrate how the class reached the overall objective of "speaking professionally"; that is, with clarity, well-organized ideas, and appropriate grammar, vocabulary and tone.

DEVELOPING METHODOLOGY, CONTENT AND LANGUAGE SKILLS

While none of the syllabuses described so far sets out a methodology, methodology, content and language skills are often interwoven in commercially produced materials for workplace classes.

Elsa Auerbach and Nina Wallerstein developed *ESL for Action: Problem-Posing at the Workplace* to promote education for change. This problem-posing methodology is based on the Freirian model, which starts from the experiences of workers' own lives. From these experiences, the teacher chooses relevant themes that serve as the basis for building a critical consciousness, leading finally to informed action.

According to Auerbach and Wallerstein, the goal of problem-posing is "critical thinking and action, which starts from perceiving the social, historical, or cultural causes of problems in one's life. But critical thinking continues beyond perception—toward the actions and decisions people take to gain control over their lives. As a group process, problem-posing enables people to see social connections, rather than blame themselves for having difficulty 'making it'...and to gain self-confidence to act outside the classroom to make changes in their lives."

In each chapter of their book, a problem-posing methodology guides the development of tasks that explore workplace issues. This methodology has three phases:

- Listening (or investigating the issues of the community).
- Dialogue (or codifying issues into discussion "codes" for critical thinking).
- Action (or developing strategies for making the changes students envision following reflection).

For instance, they divide a unit on health and safety into the following five lessons:

- A Safe Workplace

BUSINESS LANGUAGE COURSE
ORAL PROFICIENCY

Sept. 22   *Group Needs Assessment*

Sept. 29   *Telephone Talk*: Establishing rapport, rate of speech, techniques for effective calls, energy on the phone, improving your tone, controlling your voice, going out of your way for the caller. Role-play. Some idioms.

Oct. 6   *Speaking Professionally*: What would you say? Saying the right thing when you don't know what to say: playing for time, responding to the negative, accepting and giving compliments, etc. Discourse markers, organizing your thoughts. Individual mini-presentations.

Oct. 13   *Small Talk and Active Listening*: Saying the right thing. Telephone talk. More idioms.

Oct. 20   *Simulation*: Feedback and analysis of participation.

Oct. 27   *Assigning and Planning Individual Presentations*: Articulate your topic. Elements of and guidelines for presentations. A lexical set (new words).

Nov. 3   *Pronunciation Clinic*: Speaking smoothly, word stress, sentence stress, intonation. *Grammar Clinic*: Correcting mistakes versus errors, active and passive voice, simple and continuous aspect. Mid-course evaluation.

Nov. 10   *Prepare Talk Show*: Establishing rapport, speaking like an expert, active listening, giving opinions and taking the floor, speaking expressively (guests, hosts, commercials?). Practice run.

Nov. 17   *Talk Show*: You're on the air. Self-evaluation.

Nov. 24   *Presentations and Feedback*: Four 30-minute presentations, 10-minute feedback for each.

Dec. 1   *Presentations and Feedback*: Four 30-minute presentations, 10-minute feedback for each.

Dec. 8   *Presentations and Feedback*: Four 30-minute presentations, 10-minute feedback for each. Give out end-of-course evaluations.

Dec. 15   *Presentations and Feedback*: Four 30-minute presentations, 10-minute feedback for each. End-of-course evaluations. Wrap-up.

Adapted from material provided by Valerie Hickey, Multicultural Workplace Program, Continuing Education, Board of Education for the City of Toronto, Ontario.

- Hazards in the Workplace
- Acting for Health and Safety
- After an Accident or Illness
- Pregnancy on the Job

In each lesson, the three steps move the learners through the process of identifying problems, analysing the situations and taking action. Activities planned for each step incorporate important, relevant content with practice in skills, grammar and vocabulary.

A similar three-step process drawn from a literacy approach popular in Central America shapes the materials developed by Deborah Barndt, Mary Ellen Belfiore and Jean Handscombe in *English at Work: A Tool Kit for Teachers*. In each of the five units included in this book, the methodology involves describing, analysing and then acting upon experiences. This three-step process structures the sequence of activities in each unit so that learners move from the familiar to the analytical to the planned action. The descriptive stage is called "scratching the surface." The second is titled "digging deeper" and the third "making your own tool."

As outlined on the chart on the following page, each unit suggests a specific learning tool or medium. The participants use the tool co-operatively to explore the content of the unit by identifying the problem situations, analysing them, and developing solutions designed to bring about change. The tool also helps teachers and learners complete their own needs analyses and serves as a model for developing their own learning materials.

The objectives of each unit are clearly categorized according to content, language and methodology as indicated in the following example drawn from a unit on work relationships:

Content Objectives

- To focus on communication situations between workers and supervisors, workers and the public, workers and other workers.
- To better understand some of the social and psychological factors that affect these relationships.

Language Objectives

- To develop listening skills that will lead to greater comprehension.
- To practise the language needed to confront difficult communication situations.
- To develop oral reading fluency among native speakers.

Methodology Objectives

- To use the tape recorder—for both collecting workers' stories and for practising listening, speaking, etc.
- To experiment with a radio novel—a workers' radio show in soap opera form—and to explore its further use in teaching language and literacy skills.

THEME	TOOL	TECHNIQUE	CONTENT
Our Histories as Immigrant Workers	Oral Histories (Stories)	Workers' stories to make learning materials	Personal immigration histories Comparing jobs there and here Contribution of immigrant workers to the economy
Our Jobs within Overall Production (or Service) Process	Photo Packages (Photographs)	Photographs to stimulate identification, motivate discussion, develop sequences and make stories	Job descriptions, tasks, language needs on the job Steps in job routines and the production process Communication networks and decision-making structure within the workplace
Our Work Relationships (with Management, the Public, Other Workers, Union)	Radio Novels	Taped radio novel to involve students actively in listening to and practising dialogues	Relations with supervisors, coworkers, clients and the public Union participation
Our Working Conditions	Cartoon Card Game	Drawings and caricatures to stimulate identification, storytelling, analysis	Wages and benefits Health and safety Training and educational opportunities
Impact of Our Work on Home and Community Life	Day in the Life (Poster)	Posters to provide visual focus Photo sequence to develop narrative skills	Links between work and home/community life Double day and child-rearing Community activities

Adapted with permission from *English at Work: A Tool Kit for Teachers* by D. Barndt, M.E. Belfiore and J. Handscombe. Syracuse, N.Y.: New Readers Press, 1991.

Tool

■ The tool is an audio tape of the radio show *As the World Works*, which includes a series of different interactions between workers and supervisors, the public and fellow workers. A cassette tape recorder is required for listening to the radio novel and for recording your own in class.

The methodology objectives shown in this example relate to the "tool"—the audio tape—that brings a concrete perspective to the unit. The overall methodology—scratching the surface, digging deeper and making your own tool (in other words, description, analysis and action) structures the sequence of activities.

This fundamental structure is also reflected in the needs analysis. As we are conducting the needs analysis, we look for communication problems that are evident in the way language is used. At the same time, we are building relationships within the sponsoring organizations.

Once specific communication needs have been identified, they can be treated in the context of the larger framework. "Calling in sick," for example, can be included in a section on problems related to health and safety or to home and family life. Are people frequently off work because of conditions on the job, because of family responsibilities or, more likely, a combination of the two? In class, learners practise the steps involved in phoning in sick so they become competent at this specific task, which falls under the overall objective of following through on a process of enquiry and problem-solving.

The method used to teach and learn can therefore guide how we order and treat the content of the course. In *Educating for a Change*, Rick Arnold, Bev Burke, Carl James, D'Arcy Martin and Barb Thomas build their teaching around "the spiral model," illustrated here, which integrates reflection and action.

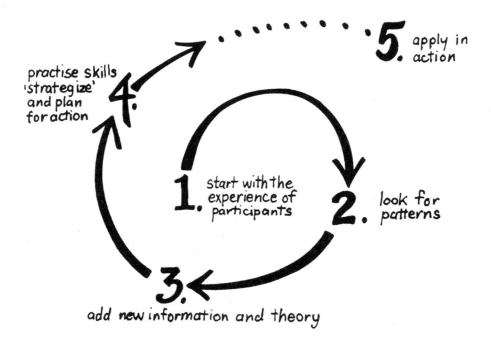

According to the authors, this model suggests that:

- Learning begins with the experience or knowledge of the participants.
- After participants have shared their experience, they look for patterns or analyse the experience (how are their experiences alike and how are they different?).
- To avoid being limited only to the knowledge or experience of people in the room, they also collectively add or create new information or theory.
- Participants need to try on what they've learned: to practise new skills, make strategies and plan for action.
- Afterwards, when they return to their workplace, they apply what they've learned in the workshop.

In an advanced communication course in an accounting firm, the teacher used the description, analysis and application methodology over a six-month period. She presented each section of the syllabus on the following page at supervisors' meetings and again at the final evaluation. The course objectives were organized according to skill areas and the activities drew on situations familiar in both work and community life. The objectives were drawn up co-operatively, through class discussion and individual needs assessments. As the course progressed, new objectives and activities were added to complement the growing interest of participants.

One of the main goals of this course was to improve oral communication with colleagues and clients. The participants identified the following oral skills they wanted to focus on:

- Handle client complaints and questions more confidently on the telephone.
- Participate more actively at department meetings.
- Make presentations about work initiatives and results to a large group, including supervisors and managers.

The three-step process for improving presentation skills, for example, began with role-plays of difficult work experiences involving clients and colleagues. Through discussing and revising the role-plays, new solutions were tried out. Then, the participants gave short tours of their own work stations, describing their work to colleagues in other departments.

At the analysis stage, the presentations took on a multicultural perspective as participants presented historical, political, cultural, religious and geographical snapshots of their home countries. This involved research, organizing ideas and giving in-depth responses to questions.

In the final stage, the participants tackled work-related presentations at company meetings. The workplace classroom became a laboratory for practising and assessing the forthcoming presentations. In a follow-up class, the presentation made at the company meeting was reviewed and evaluated by the class.

At each stage of the process, learners were required to handle more demanding tasks and more sophisticated content. At the first stage, they dealt with familiar work tasks; at the second, they moved on to research and analysis; and at the third, their

OBJECTIVES AND ACTIVITIES

OVERALL OBJECTIVE

To improve oral and written communication through observing, analysing, practising and monitoring progress in the following areas that have been identified as needing improvement:

SPECIFIC OBJECTIVES	ACTIVITIES

Description

Speaking and Listening

Explaining problems and relaying information	Role-play of real experiences
Communicating in a group	Small- and large-group presentations
■ Speaking up at meetings	■ Tours of worksites
■ Making presentations	■ Video/simulation
Communicating on the telephone	Role-play of real experiences
■ Responding to unpredictable requests	■ Live taping
■ Convincing, explaining	

Reading and Writing

Identifying writing tasks that need attention or improvement (memo, letter, report)	Bring in samples of work or work in progress
	■ Weekly journals

Analysis

Speaking and Listening

Exploring the multicultural context	Country talks
Discussing and analysing issues	News articles
Communicating in a group	Role-plays
■ Explaining, describing and responding to work information	

Reading and Writing

Reading complex information for understanding	News articles
Summarizing information	Work information
Enhancing writing skills	Writing responses to news articles
	Job descriptions, grammar exercises

Application

Speaking and Listening

Communicating in a group	Presentations lab
■ Organizing information	Discussions and readings
■ Interacting in a group discussion	Role-plays of real experiences
■ Fielding questions	
Communicating on the telephone or in person	
Pronunciation, grammar	Performance assessment forms
	Individual work

Reading and Writing

Recognizing organization markers	Readings: Columbus, cross-cultural and cross-gender communication, cultural communities
Making inferences, integrating information	
Developing writing style, vocabulary, grammar	Performance assessment forms
	Grammar exercises

Adapted with permission from *English at Work: A Tool Kit for Teachers* by D. Barndt, M.E. Belfiore and J. Handscombe. Syracuse, N.Y.: New Readers Press, 1991.

presentations included both descriptive and analytical information and were judged by their colleagues, supervisors and managers.

LOOKING AHEAD TO ACTIVITIES

The language level of the class or group, identified in the needs analysis, usually determines the content that needs to be emphasized or explored in depth. For instance, let's break down the communication techniques involved in teaching and learning how to request time off. To perform this task, learners must be able to:

- Identify days of the week and dates.
- Identify times of day and hours.
- Ask for time to talk to the supervisor.
- Make the request.
- Give reasons for the request.
- Understand and respond to the supervisor's hesitancy. Persuade.
- Understand and respond to either the supervsior's refusal or acceptance of the request.
- Express appropriate thanks or regrets.
- End the conversation.

In this situation, identifying days of the week, dates and times would probably be emphasized in a basic-level class, while an advanced group would deal with some of the more complex issues related to this task. A variety of communication activities, games and exercises can be used to provide practice in the various aspects of the overall task.

For example, if a special event is being planned in class (a speaker, party, visitor, etc.), learners might be given a calendar and invited to work in twos or threes to determine which day would be best. The language used can be as simple as:

"Is Tuesday a good day?"
"Which Tuesday?"
"January 12."
"No, I'm busy. I'm going to the doctor."

For the remaining communication items (making the request, giving reasons, responding to the answer), we can use easier listening and speaking exercises that introduce one or two formula phrases such as, "Could I...?"

In an intermediate class, we could explore various ways of structuring the request, project the supervisor's responses and, in case the response is no, examine how the request might be presented more persuasively. For instance, learners might listen to two taped dialogues, one in which the worker gets a positive response to a request for a day off and the other in which the response is negative. In small groups, they can then try to identify two or three uses of language that account for the response. They can be instructed to listen to how the conversation begins, the tone of voice of the supervisor (friendly, busy, angry), the actual phrasing of the request and the substance of the reasons given. Once they've done this, invite them to rewrite the negative dialogue and present their version to the class, which then decides whether it's likely to be successful.

While the teaching and learning objectives for basic and intermediate classes are often very similar, the depth in which the material is explored is usually quite different. The same objective can be set for both a basic and intermediate class, though more difficult tasks are assigned to learners in the advanced group.

When a class includes learners whose English-language proficiency is mixed, they can be divided into groups according to their language level and the groups can be assigned different tasks.

When designing a syllabus, we select and organize content, usually in co-operation with the learners and the sponsors. As language teachers, we operate within the broad framework of communication, integrating our knowledge of the workplace and the community with the language skills required to function in both environments. In educating for change, we place learners' communication needs within a framework that encourages critical thinking and informed, confident action.

CHAPTER 6 Developing Materials for Classroom Use

Developing materials for use in the classroom is one of the most exciting, yet demanding, opportunities workplace programs provide—for both teachers and learners. The individuality of each workplace environment, the specific demands of the sponsor(s) and the unpredictability of learners' needs, interests and abilities mean that a single textbook is unlikely to be appropriate for use in all situations or to meet the various needs that become evident as the course progresses. Nevertheless, some commercially produced materials may be useful in certain circumstances.

For instance, a group that needs to work on pre-literacy reading or writing skills or practise pronunciation may benefit from following a prescribed course for a specified period during each class. In mixed-level classes, using commercially produced materials helps reduce some of the preparation time the teacher must put in when coping with learners at different skill levels. Usually, however, workplace teachers are responsible for integrating the sponsor's demands, the learners' expectations and the educational institution's requirements into materials that are individually tailored to each class.

This chapter will examine a variety of materials—authentic materials drawn from the workplace and the community, some commercially prepared materials, and materials produced by the learners themselves. In all three instances, the tasks that we design to help learners interact with the material—to understand it, comment on it and enquire beyond it—are crucial. Tasks and activities are developed to achieve the objectives we have defined for the course, whether these are job-specific functional objectives or problem-posing objectives that define a method of enquiry.

ACCOMMODATING THE LEARNING ENVIRONMENT

Before looking at examples of materials, let's examine the learning environment of workplace settings more closely. The characteristics of a particular environment influence the materials we use and the lessons we design. While the learners may have a variety of needs, interests and English language skills, a single employer and a single union often provide common factors.

Unfortunately, however, this is not always the case. In large companies, workers may be represented by several unions. In other cases, a variety of stakeholders, including employers, unions and the community, may form a consortium or a co-operative group to provide educational opportunities for workers. One example is Skillplan in British Columbia, which was set up by and for the construction industry. Another example is Peterborough Workplace Education in Ontario, which facilitates partnerships in learning in a variety of area workplaces.

In a class made up of people from different departments who do not know each other or the jobs they do, teachers can capitalize on the fact that they all work for the same employer. We can invite learners to describe their jobs and relate them to the overall production process. In some instances, the class may be able to tour the worksite so that each person can describe the work he or she does. This works particularly well in large industries, corporate settings, hospitals and hotels where workers are more likely to come from different departments. Not only are people interested in what their coworkers do, but they also take pride in explaining their own responsibilities to others. This kind of activity is especially effective for building self-confidence and developing a sense of community in the class by encouraging mutual respect.

When planning workplace classes, teachers must keep in mind a number of factors that may influence the learning environment.

FATIGUE

If classes are scheduled at the end of the work day, learners are almost certain to be tired. Transition activities can help them relieve this end-of-the-day fatigue and adjust to the change of pace from work. Some teachers use short physical exercises to ease the transition. Others provide a few minutes for refreshments so that people can reorient themselves and socialize before they tackle concentrated learning.

IRREGULAR ATTENDANCE

Irregular attendance is another factor to consider when planning the program. This problem is often more pronounced when teachers are provided to the employer free-of-charge and when employees attend classes entirely on their own time. Because the employer has made no financial commitment to the program in these situations, the teacher often has no lever to encourage management or learners to maintain their enthusiasm for the program.

In factories, layoffs, overtime and shiftwork often mean that attendance may vary from 12 people one week to three or four the next. In office settings, routines are often upset by the pressure to complete unanticipated work. In one financial institution, for instance, not only were the telephone staff often told to skip class to keep up with their workload but supervisors were also called out to attend to problems.

Learners' responsibilities at home can also affect attendance, especially when classes are on workers' own time. In these situations, teachers can introduce practices to counteract the potentially demoralizing effect of dwindling attendance. Those who attend the classes regularly can be responsible for keeping their coworkers up-to-date. Peer pressure is often more effective than teacher pressure in encouraging people to return to class. Those who rotate days or shifts might come to class on their days off or, with the permission of the employer, workers who have been laid off may be encouraged to continue attending the class.

As teachers, we can take our concerns about attendance to the employer or the union or both. A teacher conducting a program at a financial institution, for example, spoke with the manager of the project, reiterating the need for regular attendance and suggesting that other staff cover for learners who were in class. The manager agreed and the class proceeded with more visible management support.

UNEXPECTED ISSUES ARISING FROM THE JOB

While teachers can never anticipate at the planning stage all the issues that may arise, we can expect the unexpected by remaining flexible and thinking of a lesson as a complete unit containing a number of tasks. It isn't unusual for learners to arrive at class with their attention focused on an event that happened on the job (e.g., a reprimand, layoff notice or incorrect payslip). We can take advantage of their interest by relating the issue to the tasks that had originally been planned. Or it may be possible to relate it to another task that we had intended to cover later on. For instance, if there is a misunderstanding about shift changes, we may deal with it in class by building on work we've already done with time and days of the week. Describing the problem and exploring the causes, solutions and various forms requests may take can provide a model for helping learners deal with other similar tasks, such as requesting time off. This kind of flexibility, which often involves reviewing and recycling topics and tasks, can help learners who have missed a few classes practise material covered in their absence.

MIXED LEVELS

Because the number and range of classes in workplace programs are often limited, it usually isn't possible to group learners homogeneously. Even in a basic class, for example, there is often a mix of language competence. Some learners may need literacy or even pre-literacy training while others may be able to cope with written English at a basic level.

In an intermediate class, the level of learners' oral skills may be fairly consistent, but there may be a wide range of competence in reading and writing. This was precisely the situation in a course for municipal workers. Although the learners' reading skills were fairly similar, their writing skills varied widely. Two men had never tried to write in English, while others were responsible for writing reports.

Group work is an effective way of handling this kind of diversity. For example, oral work on reporting an accident could include small group discussions on the kinds of accidents that occur frequently, why they occur and how they are reported. Following up these discussions by assigning different writing tasks tailored to the ability of each groups works effectively.

Learners who want to practise writing extended prose could write up an accident report either as a group or individually, then exchange reports. Basic-level writers could be invited to fill in an accident report form with a one-sentence description of what happened. If the company's accident form is complicated, these learners could fill in only certain sections, or they could work with a simplified teacher-prepared form like the following, which was adapted from a company form:

ACCIDENT REPORT

NAME _____

DEPARTMENT _____

TIME of accident _____

LOCATION of accident _____

DESCRIBE briefly what happened _____

TYPE OF INJURY _____

Did worker go to hospital? _____

Learners whose skills are more advanced could be enlisted to help others, encouraging participants to depend on their peers rather than the teacher.

AUTONOMY

Equally as important as encouraging learners to develop a healthy peer dependence is fostering the development of autonomy and independent learning strategies that they can apply beyond the classroom. Because workplace programs are part-time and usually shorter than adult intensive courses, the need to encourage autonomy is heightened. This can be achieved by acknowledging the rich experience of learning that adults already possess—both in and out of the classroom—and by building on this experience to help them grow in knowledge and skills.

Course participants can also learn how to assess their own progress and evaluate the course's effectiveness in meeting their needs, thus developing their own analytical and critical skills and helping the teacher tailor the course to their perceived needs.

LANGUAGE FOR INTERACTION

If we view meaningful, appropriate communication as the primary function of language, then our classroom practice should present language as communication and stress the interaction between communicators in getting across meaning. For example, in developing a lesson about requesting time off, we can shift learners' focus from grammatical accuracy or formula phrases (Could I...? Would it be possible...?) to deciding who they are talking to, understanding the difficulty or ease of fulfilling their request, and predicting the response.

At the intermediate level, learners can talk about whether their supervisors are easy or difficult to get along with and when the best time is to catch them in a good mood. If this direct approach is not suitable in a specific workplace, we can pick up on learners' spontaneous comments about their supervisors or simply generalize about people's moods—what affects them, how they're influenced by stress and so on. Learners can also discuss the likelihood of getting time off, which often depends on the workload at a particular time of year, the number of other employees on holidays, the stability of the company, etc. With these factors in mind, what kind of request do they want to make?

The teacher's role is to provide learners with the language they need for the task they want to perform. Before learners actually role-play the situation themselves, they can listen to some simulated taped dialogues, in which some requests are successful and others are not. They might try to predict the outcomes based on the participants' tone of voice, hesitancy, reactions, etc. Analysing these dialogues will help them be more sensitive when they produce their own.

As they develop their own role-play, class members should be encouraged to pursue questions such as, "What did you really mean here?" or "Why did you say it that way? Are you angry with her?" This helps learners look critically at the language they have produced. If this activity is carried out in small groups, the groups can compare their dialogues, acknowledging variety but making sure the responses are sensible and appropriate.

In this example, the task is not to come up with the right response, but to go through the process of negotiating meaning to produce an appropriate response that communicates meaning in context—a more open-ended task. At this level, we are encouraging learners to discover independently how language is used—good practice for life-long learning.

Realistically, learners at the basic level cannot talk in detail about a situation like this unless the class is bilingual. Yet even at this level, we can emphasize the importance of context by preparing exercises that present requests in two different situations. For example, appropriate language for making requests can be introduced by contrasting pictures or brief stories of a social situation with the work situation. Do the workers have coffee breaks together and do they socialize? If so, one request involving peers (e.g., getting a coffee, the latest sports results, asking where something was bought) could be presented in this context. Requests involving the employer and the employee (e.g., time off, clarification, assistance) can also be presented.

Perhaps there are people in the class who can take a stab at making the request. Their ideas—and ours—can introduce the variety of contexts in which language is used.

If possible, the class can be divided into groups and one group can suggest more situations for another group to talk about and determine the appropriate form for the request. In this situation, learners are in a sense creating the materials by identifying the situations that are most immediate for them. Even though learners at this level do not have a wide repertoire of language to work with, the task encourages them to analyse the situation before deciding what to say.

If language involves communicating meaning and a process of analysing and developing creative solutions, then our classrooms should enable the learners to practise this. Rather than presenting learners with pre-scripted dialogues to read to each other, create a dialogue with them by focusing on meaning rather than form. In this way, we encourage learners to think about what they want to say, who they want to talk to and how it might be said. Oral interactions do not exist in isolation but are part of a context involving knowledge and emotions. See Classroom Sequence 2 in Chapter 7 for a description of how a teacher can develop an unscripted dialogue with basic-level learners.

Focusing on meaning rather than form helps present language not as a closed system of rules and behaviours but rather as a dynamic, interactive communication tool. When we talk to other people, for instance, we are constantly interpreting what we hear so that we can respond and choose how to say things. As native English speakers, we are thoroughly conditioned to cope with this unpredictability, but learners must recognize and develop the confidence to do the same. Learning language as communication is learning to operate in a dynamic situation in which we are continuously thinking about what is being said and deciding how to respond. If we view language as an open, dynamic system, then the teaching and learning situations we create should reflect this.

SOURCE MATERIALS

Photographs, tape-recorded interactions and a variety of printed materials provide excellent classroom resources for workplace programs. Depending on the specific communication needs identified at the needs analysis stage, teachers can gather materials and use them to develop learning tasks.

PHOTOGRAPHS

Suppose the supervisors in a small manufacturing plant comment that they often feel that their instructions regarding production are not understood. Because following instructions requires an understanding of context, photographs of the entire production process can be used to help learners see where their particular job fits in.

With an intermediate level class, a small group might be asked to identify the steps in the production process and note the ones they are involved in. Then they might compare the steps that are already familiar with those shown in the photos to ensure that every important step has been covered. Naming the steps involves using technical vocabulary and sequencing markers, such as "first," "then" and "after that."

When learners are less advanced, we could invite them to organize the photos in sequence before moving on to oral work that would involve naming the various steps. We can check how much of this vocabulary they already know by working orally with the whole class or with learners in small groups. To fill in the rest, we could ask a worker whose English skills are more advanced to review the process with them so that they use listening skills to complete the task. In this situation, learners would listen only for the specific information they need. Techniques for requesting repetition and clarification could be practised beforehand, so that important information is not missed.

If it becomes obvious that placing the stages of the production process in sequence or naming the various stages needs to be reviewed, the photos can be used in a variety of ways. For example, short sentences or even a single word can be cut up and scrambled. Working alone or in groups, learners can then be invited to match the sentences with the sequenced photos. Or, if learners form pairs, one person might silently read a description of a step, then describe it to the partner in her or his own words so that the partner can select the correct picture.

In these examples, the photos are the key to devising tasks that integrate a variety of skills—listening, speaking and reading. The tasks are interrelated and the skills involved follow a natural progression, such as oral to reading or oral to writing. They may also follow a sequence such as identifying, matching, copying and placing in sequence independently.

Photographs can also be used to identify parts of machines, tools or materials that are being processed. Learners can produce their own list of parts, tools, materials or safety equipment by referring to the photos. If their technical vocabulary is limited, try asking them to write simple descriptions that contain the basic names (e.g., The wire connects to.... Gloves protect....). Then, by reading and looking at the pictures, the learners can identify the object and its name and record this on a list.

The workers probably know the names of the parts of the machine that break down and the tools that often need repair; in other words, the items on the list that create problems for them. They may not, however, be aware of all the safety equipment that is available or required as pictured in the photos.

Naming various items may not be difficult, but the overall objective is to help learners understand instructions that incorporate these names and relate these to the entire job process. Integrating the photos into a sequence of tasks that depends on completing one step before the next can be tackled successfully helps achieve this purpose. Naming the items, for example, is a prerequisite for identifying the problem areas. Once the problem areas are identified, they might become the focus of more concentrated work on giving and following instructions.

In *English at Work: A Tool Kit for Teachers*, Deborah Barndt, Mary Ellen Belfiore and Jean Handscombe provide six packages of work-specific photos and worksheets. The tasks in the worksheets begin with descriptive exercises (naming, placing in sequence, identifying, giving reasons), then move on to analytical and action-oriented activities. In the analytical phase, photos are used in several ways to help learners develop their critical thinking skills:

- Locating their jobs within the overall production process.
- Comparing jobs on the basis of tasks, pay, hours, requirements, etc. This task highlights the differences between so-called men's and women's work, between manual jobs and desk jobs, etc.
- Examining the materials of production. Where do the materials come from? Are they raw or finished? Do any of the workers come from the countries where these materials originate?
- Connecting the product to the producer. Can the workers afford to buy the product they produce?

TAPE-RECORDED INTERACTIONS

In some workplace situations, teachers are able to record authentic conversations (with permission) as they take place on the shop floor, over the telephone, in the supervisor's office or at meetings. If conversations relevant to the identified needs are taped, then we have an invaluable resource for analysing interactions.

In one workplace, for example, the supervisor communicated with workers mostly by telephone because of the variety of work locations. He had identified problems with listening comprehension directly related to enquiries, instructions and reports communicated over the telephone. He agreed to have some of his conversations taped so they could be used in class. In each case, the worker involved was also asked for permission.

Tasks based on tapes like this could involve listening for specific information (e.g., location, time, names, specific requests, orders), for sequence, for changes in tone of voice or simply for getting the drift of the conversation. We might begin by asking the class what is communicated in these telephone conversations (reports, enquiries, instructions) and record their comments on a chalkboard or flip chart. Does their list match the supervisor's? What does a report or enquiry include?

The learners could role-play a few conversations to identify the kind of information related in each of these conversations. Can they identify which interactions cause problems? If so, the class could start with these conversations. Perhaps they don't feel there are any comprehension problems. Do the tapes confirm this perception? Whether they do or not, the teacher can prepare the learners to listen by starting with oral work that draws on the learners' knowledge and perceptions of situations and problems.

Worksheets based on the tapes can be prepared so that small groups can work together to analyse the conversations. If the learners' English skills are mixed, tasks at varying levels of difficulty can be assigned to different groups. A less advanced group might be able to get only a few points of specific information and the general drift of the message. For instance, if the message involves a reminder about a forthcoming health and safety meeting with some information about the agenda, a worksheet for basic learners might look like this:

GETTING THE DRIFT

Listen to the conversation and try to get the drift or general idea.

Is this a message about...
... a change of shift?
... a meeting?
... a holiday?

LISTENING FOR SPECIFIC INFORMATION

Now listen for the following:

Day _____

Time _____

Place _____

More advanced learners might be invited to listen to find out the sequence of the agenda. By providing them with a worksheet like the following, which contains the sequence markers used in the conversation, we can help them focus on filling in the content of the message when they hear the cue:

AGENDA

First _____

After that _____

The last thing _____

If we prepare a sequence or chain of tasks, completing each task successfully can depend on understanding the information conveyed in the previous one. In dealing with the information about the meeting, for example, an advanced group might pass on the agenda information in their own words to the basic group.

The basic group can listen to the tape again to confirm what they have written on their worksheets. If a written bulletin is available, both groups might use it to check all the information they have heard and recorded. Or, the advanced group might draw up a written bulletin and pass it on to the basic group for checking.

If we then focus on the points that indicate whether communication has been successful or broken down, we can progress from listening to speaking. The specific content of the tapes will help us decide what to highlight.

Here are the kinds of questions teachers can use to help guide a discussion of the content of the taped material:

- Is there an obvious breakdown in communication? What is said to indicate this?
- Does the listener use any strategies to compensate for faulty comprehension, such as requests for clarification, repetition, paraphrasing, etc.?
- How does the listener indicate that the information is understood and will be acted upon? By repeating the important point to confirm? Does saying "okay" indicate thorough understanding?
- Does the speaker's tone of voice change to indicate impatience, anger, confusion, etc.? What was said and how was it said to cause this abrupt change?

By guiding an analysis of the conversation through a series of successive steps, teachers can help learners focus their efforts on interpreting the meaning of what was said.

Initially, for example, they might establish the context of the conversation by identifying the communicators, their status, the location and the topic. Then, working in groups, they can revise the conversations so that the communication is successful and appropriate. In this sequence of tasks, learners first identify and describe the problem. They then analyse the causes of the communication problem and, working together, suggest solutions. Their own revised conversation—which can be recorded—then becomes the subject of a similar analysis.

When authentic conversations are not available (e.g., if company personnel are not willing or able to co-operate in making tapes), they can be simulated. Try recruiting coworkers who are native English speakers to help prepare a tape that simulates a conversation. For example, if informal socializing at work poses problems, establish the setting (lunchroom, break time), the players (a native English speaker and a non-native English speaker) and the topic (bingo, what happened on the weekend, etc.) and encourage the participants to carry on independently. Or try pairing a native English speaker with a class member, or an advanced learner with someone whose English skills are at a basic level. Make sure they understand the setting and have the necessary information to communicate, but don't script the conversation. See how it develops spontaneously and use the language that results.

PRINTED MATERIALS

At the needs analysis stage, teachers usually acquire a variety of printed materials such as those outlined in Chapter 4. While much of the material may provide only background information about how the company or union operates, some of it may be useful for developing learning tasks. Job descriptions, for instance, often describe responsibilities in terms of activities, tools or materials used and possible hazards on the job.

Job descriptions can be used to develop learning tasks aimed at describing the sequence of the job process and responding to enquiries about the quality of work. Because many workers never get an opportunity to read their own job descriptions, they are often surprised to find discrepancies between what is described and what they actually do. It is for precisely this reason that companies are sometimes reluctant to provide written descriptions for use in workplace programs. The company may be demanding more of its workers than is actually stated in the official job description.

When job descriptions are available, however, learners can start by defining their jobs orally, then compare this to the written description. If discrepancies crop up, the process of enquiry can continue by identifying tasks that are not included in the job description and establishing reasons the workers are expected to perform them.

The outcomes of activities like this will vary, but they will give individual learners an opportunity to find a resolution that satisfies them, whether this is acceptance of the discrepancy, a request for a pay increase, consultation with colleagues or with the union, etc. When issues like this arise, it is important to remember that both the teacher and the learners must consider the possible and probable consequences of the proposed resolutions to the problem. For instance, if the worker involved decides to complain, is he or she adequately protected?

> In one workplace program, management, the union and the workers had iden-tified reading and writing skills as an area of emphasis. One commonly stated reason for this was the need for workers to develop these skills in order to receive promotions. Management was interested in promoting from within the ranks, the union wanted to protect workers' security and the workers themsel-ves wanted promotions to achieve better working conditions and higher sal-aries. The positions in question required more reading and writing on the job and, in order to be considered for promotion, workers were required to score a passing grade on a variety of written tests. Because they had been unable to complete the tests successfully in previous attempts, learners expressed a need and desire to practise test-taking and working under pressure.
>
> Although the teacher was able to look briefly at some of the tests, she was not able to use them in the class. As a result, she developed activities for the class based on the format of the tests she had seen.
>
> For example, she began by selecting a reading on artificial respiration from the company's own safety manual and developed a series of multiple-choice questions based on the content of the reading.
>
> In the past, this teacher would probably have begun an exercise like this by presenting difficult vocabulary from the reading, either questioning the class about the meanings of the words or simply giving their meanings. Then the class would have been invited to read the passage silently or aloud. Finally, the learners would have been presented with either multiple-choice questions or questions requiring simple, direct answers to test their comprehension. This methodology tests learners' comprehension, but provides them with no gui-dance in how to read for comprehension. It presents the passage in isolation, without any context except the list of vocabulary that introduced the reading. Rather than helping learners develop strategies for guessing the meanings of words from the context, the vocabulary is given to them.

This teacher knew that the learners needed more than this. To establish a context for the reading and to encourage the learners to read for meaning, she began by discussing artificial respiration with the class. One class member had taken a short course several years ago and described the steps accurately. Although the language he used was quite different from the description in the reading, it served as a totally accessible introduction to the topic. As a result, most of the learners were able to guess at the meaning of the words in the reading (e.g., pinch, nostril, airway) by thinking about what they had just heard and referring to the accompanying pictures. They then completed the multiple-choice exercise.

In this particular reading, the second part of the passage set out and illustrated the steps involved in giving artificial respiration. Once the learners had finished reading, the teacher cut up a copy of this part of the passage and invited the learners to match the pictures and explanations. Later, she presented them with a scrambled set of pictures and explanations and asked them to organize them in sequence. As a follow-up, she could have invited a first-aid group to help them practise real artificial respiration.

By presenting the passage this way, the teacher helped learners not only develop their reading and test-taking skills but also discover information in their manuals that they had never read before.

Print materials produced by the company and the union can also be incorporated into basic literacy training. When basic literacy needs are the primary motivator for requesting a program, there will probably be some specific items that learners must become acquainted with. For example, in the hospital program described in Chapter 2, the dietary staff were assigned new responsibilities that involved reading menus. When new ordering and repair-reporting procedures were introduced in a hotel, the housekeepers became responsible for filling out forms in writing. Previously, they had made reports and ordered supplies orally.

Rather than introduce the new, unfamiliar forms immediately, which might prove overwhelming, we could begin with commonly recognized signs and symbols in the community, such as street signs and public information signs (e.g., no smoking signs). Photographs or drawings of the signs could be matched with places where they are found. Or the meaning of laundry symbols on clothing labels can be worked out by learners in small groups with vocabulary supplied by more advanced learners, if possible. Then, learners might be invited to use the international symbols to draw up their own labels for certain fabrics.

Labels and signs that are common in the workplace might include colour-coded labels on chemicals or detergents, warning signs on machines (e.g., caution, danger, hazard), door signs (e.g., employees only, visitors), etc.

Either the labels or signs themselves or photographs of them can provide initial reading material that is familiar and non-threatening to the learners. We can ask learners to go out and copy some signs from the workplace. They can bring in both those they understand and others they are not familiar with. Working in groups with worksheets to record their answers, they can explain the meanings of the signs they are familiar with and ask their peers to help them understand those they find difficult.

Activities like this encourage learners to identify their own needs and to offer assistance as well as to be instructed.

Reading material about company policies and practices obtained during the needs assessment can be used to encourage learners to develop their critical reading skills.

> In a corporate setting with an advanced class, for example, a teacher was given a pamphlet, titled Employee Involvement, which outlined company policy regarding quality management. As the course evolved, the teacher found that employees frequently brought up problems they encountered in dealing with the different management styles that existed from department to department.
>
> As a result, the teacher decided to use the company's own policy document as the basis for a reading and discussion activity. The participants were guided through the document to establish a sound understanding of the management style the company espoused. Then learners were asked to assess the management of their own departments to show how it conformed to or diverged from the stated policy. These tasks were crucial in giving the participants the knowledge to ask questions and suggest changes during department meetings and their own performance reviews.

LEARNER-PRODUCED MATERIALS

To this point, we have examined ways of using source materials obtained from the sponsoring organization or the wider community. Now, let's turn to material produced by the learners themselves and consider two points: how to elicit it and how to design learning tasks based on this material.

PHOTOSTORIES

Photostories can be records of events as they happen (e.g., a class tour of the worksite, a citizenship hearing, etc.) or a representation of daily routines (e.g., getting to work, a day in the life of..., etc.). Photostories often capture expressions, feelings and attitudes that words cannot. They can add humour, pathos or sympathy to a situation. If Anna complains about how tiring grocery shopping is, she might say, "Too heavy. I tired at home." A picture of her hefting four or five grocery bags with an expression of awkwardness or frustration on her face could evoke humour or sympathy. Not only do people relate more quickly to photos than to oral stories, but the photos also stimulate them to tell their own stories, encouraging them to use the language they know. Discussing what to photograph also provides useful language practice, particularly when describing and justifying actions.

Taking photographs of class-related events as they happen not only provides good material for subsequent class activities but also builds a sense of community in the class. Initially, the teacher might take the photographs to give people an idea of what scenes to capture—scenes that show humour, expressions of joy, puzzlement, frustration, pleasure and expressive interactions with other people. Later, the learners can easily take on this responsibility.

Compiling a photostory is an activity that can be carried out by the whole class or one or two small groups. Sometimes, the event may occur outside the work situation; for example, someone's relative may be arriving from another country or a class member may be becoming a citizen. Because getting outside the classroom is often difficult, however, another possibility is to photograph role-plays that are of particular interest.

Once the photos are developed, the teacher can create activities to accompany the story. These work especially well for practising listening, speaking and writing. Working in groups, learners can arrange the photos in sequence so the story can be retold or written. Dialogue can be added and role-plays can be developed to re-enact scenes.

Pictures that capture feelings can provide a good starting point for a discussion about cause-and-effect. We can contrast two different settings in photos (e.g., the cafeteria and the personnel office) and focus on appropriate communication in different contexts. A series of photos with a clear, logical argument within them can be used to concentrate on developing a well-supported case in a dispute.

PROBLEM-POSING ACTIVITIES

Photostories and follow-up discussions can also explore issues and problems that people are concerned about. In this respect, they offer good material for problem-posing tasks, which are useful in developing the learners' autonomy. These tasks offer learners, working in groups or as individuals, the opportunity to work through a problem by examining alternatives, learning the language necessary for following through on the process, and reaching a solution.

Problem-posing tasks share many of the same characteristics as communicative language tasks. They engage the learners actively by drawing on their previous knowledge, both content and linguistic, and on their feelings and attitudes. They operate on an interactive basis so that working through the task is a group effort requiring negotiation, analysis and evaluation even though there may be several outcomes or solutions to the task. See Chapter 5 for more information on problem-posing, especially as it is used by Elsa Auerbach and Nina Wallerstein in *ESL for Action: Problem-Posing at the Workplace*.

A book of photostories and teaching activities, *Getting There: Producing Photostories with Immigrant Women*, by Deborah Barndt, Ferne Cristall and Dian Marino, provides some good examples of materials based on this method. Immigrant women working in factories and offices and women community workers were involved in the production. *Getting There* includes two photostories of immigrant women seeking employment and also advice on and instructions for creating and using photostories in a variety of educational settings. According to the authors, photostories offer a methodology for "another way of learning," which encourages learners to analyse social structures and act together to effect change by sharing their experiences.

The activities they suggest using with the photostories guide learners through a step-by-step analysis: describing the feelings evoked by the stories, identifying a similar personal experience, recognizing other people's similar problems, analysing the causes of the problems, and coming up with suggested solutions.

For example, Gloria's story takes place on the first day she travels to her factory alone. The photostory focuses on the process of "getting there" and how her anxiety and loneliness are overcome by courage and assistance. The reading activities encourage learners to come up with their own story illustrating how they have adapted to their new environment. If Gloria's story doesn't trigger a story of their own, they are encouraged to explore their feelings further by completing statements like the following:

- I felt afraid when…
- I felt alone when…
- I felt confused when…
- I needed help to (do something)…

Discussing their responses in small groups, learners are often stimulated by the similarities or differences among them and are thus encouraged to participate. Recording a written description of one of the learners is easier after it has been explored orally.

Depending on the language levels of the learners, the writing task could take a variety of forms. With non-literate learners, teachers could write the story as it is told to them or tape it and then transcribe it later. Learners with more advanced writing skills can be asked to include how they felt, what caused them to feel this way and what the outcome was. Members of this group could exchange their writing to confirm that they have included all the necessary information. This ensures that they receive feedback and that revisions can be completed based on what both the teacher and other learners have noted.

Developing and reading photostories can help learners recount the process of dealing with problem circumstances to better understand causes and outcomes.

ORAL STORIES

Depending on the language level of the class and the purpose of the activity, learners' own spoken stories can be collected and used in a variety of ways. These stories are usually stimulated by an oral discussion on a topic of interest. The topic may come up on the spur of the moment or it may be prepared and introduced by the teacher who can recount an experience of his or her own or another learner's story, or use a picture, a newspaper article or any other aural or visual catalyst. The learners can recount an incident, a story about a period of their life or a particular experience related to the topic. It may be about their past experiences (e.g., coming to Canada, finding their first job, comparing work in their native country with work in Canada) or about today's events (e.g., dealing with a supervisor's remarks, explaining reasons for returning a faulty item to the store, etc.).

A story is different from an interview, which elicits particular information by asking specific questions. Stories can be produced in a variety of teacher-learner relationships. The teacher can work one-on-one with a learner who is producing his or her own story or with the whole class to produce a group story or a series of individual stories from different learners.

DEVELOPING STORIES WITH BASIC-LEVEL LEARNERS

Learners whose listening, speaking and literacy skills are at a basic level will probably tell their stories slowly, in simple sentences, with lots of hesitation. The teacher will probably play a strong role in eliciting the content and recording it on the chalkboard or a flip chart. There will be grammatical errors and inappropriate vocabulary.

Whether the story comes from only one person or is a group effort, we must consider our participation and the learners' in editing the story as it is being recorded in writing. If the learners are at a beginning literacy level, then it's usually best to write exactly what they say (e.g., "I home 5 o'clock."); otherwise, the authors themselves will not be able to read it.

If the learners' literacy level is a little higher, we may find that some of them suggest grammatical changes or a re-ordering of the sequence. As the transcribers, we can incorporate these changes if the speaker agrees and understands the reasons for them. In this way, we encourage the class to consider alternatives, but it is the speaker who makes the ultimate decisions. After all, we are only transcribing—not deciding—for them.

In a one-on-one situation with a learner at this level, the teacher might suggest and discuss changes, then write what the speaker feels comfortable with. It's important to keep in mind that our primary purpose in using these stories is to build self-confidence in reading and writing. Rather than requiring "correct English" from learners at this level, we must let this purpose guide our decisions on editing and transcribing. In addition, learners should understand that writing doesn't come out perfectly the first time and that editing skills are useful.

Another way of documenting a story is to use a tape recorder and then transcribe the story, once again recording the speaker's words exactly as presented. This technique works particularly well with more fluent speakers whose storytelling may be constrained if someone is writing their words as they speak. Depending on the planned use of the stories and the writing abilities of the learners, we can do all the transcribing ourselves or invite learners to help by writing all or part of their own or another person's story. This encourages learners to develop skills in editing and correcting material for themselves.

In her contribution to *Approaches to Adult ESL Literacy Instruction*, Marcia Taylor gives examples of strategies for collecting and transcribing stories with individuals and groups. She also lists and describes various activities that can be used as a basis for developing stories.

ORAL STORIES AND READING SKILLS

Once collected, the learners' stories can serve a variety of purposes. With learners at the basic literacy level, for example, the language experience approach works well because it integrates speaking, reading and writing. The teacher acts as a scribe, writing the story exactly as the learner delivers it. After writing each sentence, the teacher reads it aloud and, when the story is complete, the whole thing can be read aloud several times to help connect the written and the spoken word.

Here are some follow-up activities that can be used once learners' stories have been transcribed by the teacher:

- Photocopy the story and give each student a copy to place in a file for silent reading later.
- To practise writing, students can copy all or part of the story.
- Working with their copy of the story, students can underline all the parts they can read. This not only helps the teacher assess progress, but also demonstrates progress to the student.
- Make up a cloze exercise based on the story. (Transcribe the story, leaving blanks to represent certain words. The blanks can replace certain parts of speech, such as nouns, or be spaced regularly throughout the story. Students then read the story aloud, supplying the missing word or a substitute that makes sense in the context. This kind of exercise provides excellent practice in prediction. Students may also write their answers in the blanks, although the missing words may need to be provided—in random order—on the chalkboard to help with spelling.)
- Choose a grammatically sound sentence from the story and write it on a large strip of card. Then, write each word from the sentence on an index card, matching the number of sets of index cards to the size of the group. The teacher or a volunteer reads the sentence aloud and students match the individual words on the index cards with the master sentence, reading the completed sentence as they do so. The students can also be given a set of cards and invited to work in groups to recreate the sentence without reference to the master. These activities help learners recognize individual words and the way they are put together to form a sentence.
- The word cards can be rearranged to make new sentences, particularly if one or two extra cards using other words from the story are provided.

ORAL STORIES AND WRITING SKILLS

Some techniques for using stories to improve the writing skills of learners whose English skills are at the basic level were outlined in the previous section. Even those whose skills are more advanced, however, can benefit from working with their own oral stories. They might, for example, be invited to listen to a tape or read a transcript of their story, using this as the basis for a more structured writing exercise, such as composing an accident report, letter of complaint, newspaper article, etc. This can provide practice in organizing and editing before composing.

For example, a learner's job may include responsibility for writing accident reports, but she may have trouble organizing and expressing what she wants to say. She could begin by talking about the accident and tape-recording her description. Because learners often feel more at ease talking rather than writing about an event, their oral descriptions are likely to include more detail than the written version. The taped version can be transcribed by the teacher or the learner(s), so that the ideas and the content are down on paper.

The next step is to help the learner transform her spoken language into the appropriate written form for an accident report. To complete the accident report, she must probably follow a different format and pay more attention to grammatical accuracy, choice of vocabulary and stating her ideas coherently. If spelling is a problem, she could use the teacher's transcription as a reference. This transcription can also be used to confirm that all the important points are covered in the report.

Comparing the final report with the transcription of the oral story will help learners see some of the differences between spoken and written communications. For instance, readers may have a lower tolerance for inaccuracies in grammar, word choice and appropriateness than listeners do. A speaker also has more opportunity to clarify the misunderstandings of the listener by responding to the listener's questions and by observing how well the listener is attending and following. Realizing this, learners can then consider their own goals in speaking and writing.

To focus on speaking and telling stories, we can tape native English speakers telling stories. How do native speakers order the events of their stories? What verb tenses do they use? How do they keep the listener interested? Keeping these kinds of questions in mind, learners can listen to try to incorporate some of the native English speaker's strategies and style into their own storytelling.

In addition, a transcription of an oral story from one of the class members can be used to lead into a discussion of the causes of and the solutions to a problem that crops up in the story. Or, we can review it in preparation for reading a more detailed selection about a particular topic. Class members sometimes collect the stories and prepare booklets to document the progress of the class and the issues discussed. Or they match the stories with photos or tapes of the stories to make a multi-media production for their own use or for use by other classes. The common thread among all these uses is that the learners begin by working with their own experiences related in their own words so that they can gain the confidence and the skills to move beyond this stage.

ROLE-PLAYS

Pre-scripted dialogues may be satisfactory in situations that are so highly formalized that they are almost totally predictable. For example, buying a ticket at the movie theatre probably involves using mostly formula phrases:

"Two adults, please."
"Which movie?"
"...(name of movie)."
"$10, please."

Many situations that involve oral communication in the workplace and the community are not so predictable, however. Our relationship with the other participant as well as the outcome of our interaction are open to negotiation.

Pre-scripted dialogues are usually developed to illustrate a structure or function and often do not indicate the flow of real speech. Oral interactions involve an interplay of interpreting and expressing: a process of expressing what we want to say based on our interpretation of what we hear. We can never fully predict language in this regard, so we are always negotiating meaning, both received and produced. Unlike pre-scripted dialogues, role-plays provide a format in which the flow of real language can be captured so that learners can develop their ability to interpret, express and negotiate.

If learners play themselves rather than other characters in role-plays, then they are communicating in a situation that is as close to real life as is possible for the classroom. Playing themselves in a situation that is immediately relevant, learners can use language to express their ideas, their attitudes and their emotions—in short, they can be totally involved. It also encourages them to speak and listen as they would in their home language; that is, to listen for meaning and be attentive to the attitudes and emotions of the other person so that they can respond appropriately. As we all know, work is full of problems and very often it is these problems that people bring to class. Denise Gubbay of the Pathway Industrial Unit in Britain sees role-play as a highly effective tool for addressing these problems in a language-learning context. In her book, *Role Play: The Theory and Process of a Method for Increasing Language Awareness*, she says, "Role-play was evolved to enable the teacher to meet the students at the point of strongest motivation—the point at which they must speak or else lose self-respect; that is why it is problem-centred, not language-centred."

According to Gubbay, role-play has four objectives:

- To make people more aware that there are always two sides to a problem and to help them identify with both sides so they understand the forces at work.
- To give people information about the situation and their rights.
- To give them skills or strategies so they can use this awareness and information to influence their environment.
- To show how these skills can be extended to other situations.

Gubbay suggests that role-plays work well when the teacher is paired with a learner. In this situation, the teacher has enough control to introduce unpredictable elements, thus forcing the learner to deal with the unexpected. For example, in role-playing "calling in sick," let's suppose the worker usually talks to Louise who answers the phone. He might start out by saying, "Louise, this is...." The teacher might then say, "Sorry, this isn't Louise, she's sick today." Gubbay believes it is important to introduce unpredictable elements at an early stage in language learning. This may be disconcerting for learners at first, but once they have handled the unpredictable, their confidence increases and their performance is often more assured the next time.

Two Challenging Role-Play Methods

Gubbay has developed two methods for conducting role-plays. The first is most suitable for the less advanced learner who lacks confidence and may need to rely on a framework initially. In this scenario, the teacher and the learners build up a dialogue together. As the role-play progresses, the teacher constantly analyses the structure or flow of the dialogue in terms of language functions for the learners. At this stage, no unpredictable elements are introduced, so that learners develop an understanding and an awareness of the exchange.

Once the learners are familiar with the flow and the language of the dialogue (i.e., they can reproduce it confidently and fairly accurately), the time comes for them to experience and cope with the unexpected. The teacher introduces responses such as, "You must have the wrong number," which forces learners to cope by developing strategies to avoid a total breakdown of the conversation.

The second method works particularly well with learners whose English appears to be fluent but is really ineffective because they are not attentive to the other person's responses. This method is more challenging and places the learners under pressure at all times. Assuming that there is an understanding of how the conversation should proceed, the teacher and a learner start the role-play with no preliminary analysis or guidance. The teacher stops the role-play whenever there is a growing crisis in communication; for instance, when negative feelings are aroused. The intent of this method is to show learners that a mechanical response is not enough—they must exhibit their feelings and attitudes through language as well as understand the feelings and attitudes of the other person.

With both these methods, the focus is on learning how to get through the exchange while developing the confidence to deal with the unpredictable through analysis and practice. Learners develop strategies for coping and become better able to interpret and express the total response of an involved communicator. Gubbay's book provides a very thorough explanation of each method as well as transcripts of lessons—it's a book well-worth investigating.

ORAL PRESENTATIONS

In advanced classes, especially in the corporate sector, participants are often interested in taking a more active role in meetings and making oral presentations. The syllabus for a business course shown on page 71 is one example of a course devoted to these skills. Another syllabus for a communications course, shown on page 76, shows the activities that were used to practise communicating in a group and to develop oral presentation skills.

In each case, the development is gradual with lots of practice and critiques on short topics. Along the way, attention is focused on grammar, vocabulary, and appropriateness of the language and discourse structures selected. Ending this series of activities by making a "real" presentation is the most valuable outcome for the participants.

They can use the class as a laboratory for practising and assessing the presentation and then for reviewing their performance.

Classroom Sequence 1 in Chapter 7 follows a class through the process of developing an oral presentation with suggestions and worksheets for reviewing their work.

QUESTIONNAIRES, CHARTS AND DIAGRAMS

In supplying information for questionnaires, charts and diagrams, learners are also bringing into play their experience and knowledge of the workplace and the community. The format of these devices requires them to organize their thoughts and language so they can classify or categorize items. Simple interview questionnaires like the following are often good "get-acquainted" tools to use with a class that has adequate literacy skills. In pairs or groups of three, learners can interview each other and record the information on the chart.

NAME	ARRIVAL IN CANADA	FIRST JOB IN CANADA	JOB IN HOME COUNTRY

The topics for this chart can be provided by the teacher or the participants themselves can be invited to suggest things they want to know about each other.

Some learners may need the extra support provided by a model they can follow when asking the questions and writing the answers. If so, we can reproduce the questionnaire on the chalkboard or flip chart and interview one member of the class, asking simple questions such as, "What's your name?" "How do you spell that?" and so on. The written answers require only a few words or a date rather than sentences, reducing learners' fear that they will be asked to form complete sentences.

When gathering information of this nature, it is important to remember the use to which it will be put. Once learners have provided the information, how will it be used, transformed or integrated into future lessons?

We can ask learners to introduce the people they have interviewed to the rest of the class. As the information is presented, class members can record the information so that everyone has a class list when the lesson is over. Observing the pairs or groups interacting while they carry out this task can give the teacher an indication of their competence in a number of areas—spelling, mastery of numbers, producing and understanding questions to elicit information, etc.

Although people may work in the same factory, they often have little opportunity to get to know each other because of language and cultural barriers, shiftwork and so on. With learners with a moderate degree of oral competence in English, a simple questionnaire like the one presented earlier can often spark results that go well beyond the straightforward questions and responses.

When information for a class is collected, try looking for patterns in the results. Are most people underemployed compared to their previous work experience in their home countries? Did people arrive in Canada at roughly the same time? If this was a decade or two ago, what are they experiencing in this decade? Thinking about these kinds of questions can spark lively class discussions.

In one large workplace with multiple locations, job safety was repeatedly stressed during the needs analysis. An early questionnaire presented in class asked for more work-related information:

NAME	LOCATION	JOB TITLE	ACTIVITIES	SAFETY HAZARDS

The learners in this class came from different locations and had a wide variety of jobs. The information gathered was later pooled, typed and distributed to serve as a class list for everyone. It also served as a reference sheet when the class worked on the overall production process. When accident prevention was introduced, the questionnaire provided the source material for a task aimed at identifying hazards associated with particular jobs and suggesting methods of preventing accidents. In addition, everyone in the class referred to it when they had spelling problems with job-related vocabulary.

Diagrams can also help learners interpret their knowledge and experience by providing a visual display that is often more compelling than words. If comments about fatigue and multiple responsibilities at home and at work are frequent, we might use a diagram like the one at the top of the following page to begin exploring the causes of stress.

Learners can start by filling in their own diagrams, which involves practice in numeracy (e.g., fractions, percentages, ratios). Then, working in small groups, they can compare their diagrams to discover similar patterns. A diagram like this can become the first stage in a problem-posing activity that goes on to investigate the causes and effects of stress and concludes with suggestions for reducing stress at home and at work.

Questionnaires, charts and diagrams provide a twofold benefit: content information for the course is provided by the learners themselves; and learners are encouraged to

ACTIVITY	HOURS EACH DAY	WHERE DOES YOUR TIME GO?
Work		
Shopping		
Cooking		24 Hours
Cleaning		
Child care		
Sleeping		

read and use formats of this type. Then, when they are faced with a diagram or chart in the newspaper or work-related materials, it will be familiar.

JOURNAL WRITING

Keeping a personal journal gives participants an opportunity to write informally and freely on topics related to communication and language learning. From the intermediate level on, this practice, which involves a two-way exchange between the teacher and the individual learner, is rewarding for both. If participants are asked to concentrate their efforts on communication problems and successes, then they become involved in examining their individual performance and assessing their needs on a regular basis. Journal writing is best left untouched by the teacher's corrections of grammar and spelling; if possible, save this for other writing activities in which learners would be expected to revise content and form.

Journals should always be confidential to ensure that the writers can freely comment on their own performance as well as the progress of the class. The teacher's role is often to stimulate thoughts and writing with pertinent questions, such as the following:

■ Who did you talk to in English this week?
■ Did the person understand you or not?
■ How did you solve a communication problem?
■ How did you feel when this happened?
■ What did you think of our class on role-plays?
■ Did you discover some new ways to get out of difficult situations?

Classroom Sequence 1 in the next chapter shows how a teacher introduced journal writing to an advanced class and gives an example of her first journal entry to the whole class.

LEARNERS AS RESEARCHERS

In a sense, we encourage learners to become researchers and investigators by analysing their experience and recording the data in a particular format. We can also focus this research work on communication and language learning by encouraging learners to analyse their own needs in much the same way that we did when we completed the needs analysis. Learners with similar jobs can work together to produce their own communication network diagrams (see Chapter 4). If the course is weighted in favour of listening and speaking, their diagram can identify the people they communicate with or would like to communicate with orally. What topics does the learner talk about? What topics does the other person initiate?

Later, the teacher can help them detail the topics they itemize. If "paycheque" is mentioned with "personnel officer," we can help them identify requests and complaints. By creating their own communication diagrams, learners can begin to assess their present competence, determine their own priorities for learning, set goals and measure their progress. Along with the problem-posing activities mentioned earlier, this kind of task encourages "learner-training" to ensure that learning continues well beyond the classroom.

CHAPTER 7 Sequences from Workplace Classrooms

In this chapter, we'll visit two typical workplace classes. The scenarios described illustrate communicative activities that combine a variety of tasks, as well as some of the issues that workplace teachers—and class participants—are likely to encounter.

In the first scenario, an advanced class from the corporate sector is focusing on oral presentations when, midway through the lesson, a racist incident occurs. In the second, listening and speaking skills are the focus of a course for basic level learners who work in a hospital. In this instance, we'll see how the learners work as a whole class, in groups, in pairs and as individuals at tasks involving analysis and production. Once again, the teacher is called upon to deal with an unexpected conflict and guide the participants toward a resolution.

SEQUENCE 1

CLASS PROFILE

- Employees working on a small, intensive project in a large accounting firm: 12 class members; five men and seven women.
- Departments represented: data analysts, telephone data recorders and mailroom staff.
- Course time is shared equally between the company and the workers.

- Classes are held in a boardroom over lunch hour. Lunch, as well as a flip chart, whiteboard, overhead and other materials, are supplied by the company.
- Classes are scheduled twice a week for about five months; each class lasts two hours.
- Native languages: French (Québécois, Haitian, Moroccan, Mauritian), Tamil, Chinese, Arabic, Persian, English as a second dialect.
- Age range of class members: 22-42.
- Levels of education in native country: high school to MBA.
- Years in Canada: three years to born in Canada.

LANGUAGE LEVELS AND NEEDS

Everyone in the class is used to communicating orally in English at work and some use English at home. Two of the francophones are fluently bilingual orally and two of the men live with English-speaking partners. Two women from Sri Lanka are reticent but competent English speakers, except in some situations when they have trouble using the appropriate language. One of the francophone data recorders would like to work the telephones in English as well as in French. In fact, he is the person who requested the course, researched the workplace programs available and set the wheels in motion.

The self-confidence, sophistication of the vocabulary used and ability to organize their thoughts before they speak varies among the class members. Only a young university graduate from Iran, the most recent arrival in Canada, needs to improve his grammar, syntax and sentence structure. All the participants want to be able to make presentations at work, to speak up at meetings and hold their own in work-related group conversations. Some need to improve their informal conversational skills on the telephone and the mailroom staff want to be cross-trained for jobs in other departments.

In reading and writing, their skills vary from low intermediate to advanced. The data analysts need to write reports and letters to clients across the country. One of the data recorders has been asked to take minutes at meetings, while another is writing a report on a new system. The mailroom staff members have the weakest reading and writing skills, but their jobs do not involve a significant amount of writing. Nevertheless, they would like to improve their reading skills and feel confident about writing short letters in English for their children. With the least exposure to English, the Iranian mailroom worker would like to upgrade both his reading and writing skills so that he can eventually find a job commensurate with his level of education.

THE CLASSROOM

It's three weeks into the course and the participants have been preparing to give a tour of their work areas that will include an outline of their specific job responsibilities. Although the mailroom staff and telephone recorders are giving a group tour, the others are presenting their tours individually. So far, Len and Pierre have made their presentations and Eliana, the teacher, has been helping the class evaluate them. They have examined the structure, organization of content and use of language during the tour. Eliana has explained that class members should try to incorporate some of the suggestions for improvement in subsequent tours.

On this particular day, Eliana is putting up flip charts to review the tour process when the class members start to arrive. Lorraine comes in earlier than usual to report that she can't attend today because her supervisor told her to spend the time clearing up backlogged work. Eliana has encountered the same problem with a number of participants in this workplace and decides to investigate further. She asks Lorraine what kind of work has been piling up and whether other people cover for her while she's in class, as management promised. As a result of this conversation, Eliana decides that a talk with the supervisor and manager is necessary if absenteeism isn't to become a regular and accepted part of the program.

When everyone has assembled, Eliana first goes over the agenda for the class, which is written on the whiteboard:

Class Business: journals, scheduling of next tours
Preparation for tour: review of critical points
Tour of Gordon's workspace: presentation
Review and critique of tour: individual and small group work

Eliana has planned to introduce journal writing by reading her own initial entry to the group. She hands out journals and briefly explains their purpose. She introduces her own entry by explaining that, because participating in office meetings was a priority for everyone, she attended a department meeting as an observer and researcher. Because class members had indicated that participating in these meetings was difficult for them, she wanted to find out why. Was their status as learners of English as a second language the major reason or did other significant factors relating to the way people interacted and communicated at these meetings contribute to their reluctance? The entry she read is on the following two pages.

Class members seem enthusiastic about keeping journals, although some want errors in grammar, spelling and sentence structure corrected. Eliana is sure that once they experience the pleasure of writing freely, they will accept this aspect of journal writing. Their need for correction can be met by the other writing they do in nearly every session.

At this point, she turns to the real business of the day—"touring"—and quickly establishes who will be ready to present their workspace over the next two weeks. This settled, she directs attention to the flipcharts, which contain pointers for the tour presenters. She reminds them that, except for a few points added after the last presentation, most of this information has been talked about over the previous weeks. The information is important to both the tour presenters and the audience because they must evaluate the tour orally and in writing.

Journal Entry #1   *November 6ᵀᴴ*

 I enjoyed our first few classes-lots of humour and plenty of serious work. The best combination as far as I'm concerned.

 After class on Tuesday I sat in on one of the office meetings with the manager, supervisors and staff. I was interested in observing how the conversation and discussion was managed. For instance, who iniciated talk, how participants contributed to the discussion, who made & offered decisions and how topics were closed and the next topic taken up.

 I noticed that - instructions were given in an informal manner such as "we'll have to" or "it would be nice to have" or "you might try". There was no obvious confirmation that these instructions would be followed and no summing up.

 I also noticed that individuals were given space to speak or present or answer a question but if they weren't fast enough, someone else would answer for them. There was a consistant pattern of interruption & talking over each other, too. In general a fast pace with an interested, lively group.

 I had some questions which you might be able to answer regarding the meeting. Do participants always recognize they have jobs to do since the instructions are given informally? What would you need to do to answer questions before a supervisor or another participant jumps in?

 Now - about these journals. Once a week - on Thursdays - I'll ask you to hand me in your journal with your comments about the week. I'd like you to keep your ideas, suggestions and thoughts limited to the topic of your learning in this course and how you see it affecting your work and life. You could comment on the classes we've had or a particular work event where communication was required. Think about incidents where your communication was _successful_ as well as those times where you had problems. Try to analyse why the interaction was successful or why you had difficulty. You could mention a book you are reading or something you heard on the radio or saw on television that relates to your learning.

I will write back just a few lines on your journals and try to give you a class journal entry like this one on a regular basis. The journal is for informal writing - I won't be correcting grammar or sentence structure. It's an opportunity to reflect on what you have done over the week and to keep track of your learning. I hope it will help you evaluate your progress as you move through the course.

This was a rather long journal entry - let's keep them to _one page_ (I will too!). I look forward to reading your journals over the weeks ahead.

Eliana

Here is the material Eliana presented on the flip charts:

TOURS: POINTERS FOR PRESENTERS AND LISTENERS

Structure: Clear and explicit organization
Introduction
- Outline the topics you'll cover
Body of the talk
Call for questions
Summing up

Presentation
Define your terms
Keep checking that the audience is with you
Explain your graphics clearly
Language use:
- Use markers for organization—first, next, then, after that, etc.
- Use plain language, clear pronunciation, appropriate tone
- Be aware of grammatical and functional errors that can block comprehension or create confusion

Gordon, a data analyst, gets ready to conduct his tour while Eliana sets up the tape recorder. After each tour, she listens to the tape at home and notes strengths and weaknesses relating to structure and language. She gives each presenter a written critique to supplement the comments of the other class members. For the participants, these short tours are the first step toward achieving their goal of feeling confident about making presentations at their project meetings, when administrators from "downtown" come to find out about their work. Eliana believes the group is already making good progress.

Gordon's job is one of the most complicated to explain because there is little hands-on work to demonstrate outside of his computer and the spreadsheets he produces. Realizing that he is at a disadvantage, he has prepared a brief point-form information sheet about the function and responsibilities of his job. He is the first presenter to use this aid and the class responds positively. He also has a clear graphic to describe where he gets his information and where he sends his data analyses. In fact, this graphic includes everyone else's job because each participant is responsible for a portion of the data cycle. This is the first opportunity most of the participants have had to get an overview of the project they are working on.

Of all the class members, Gordon and Pierre, who both have post-university education in business, do the most sophisticated work on the project. Despite his education level, computer expertise and the print material he has provided, however, Gordon has trouble explaining the details of his work, defining terms that he uses every day in his analyses and answering questions in plain, simple English. He is Mauritian with Creole, Chinese, French and English in his language background. Although some of his early education was in English, he has difficulty following group conversations and responding to questions. In addition, his pronunciation sometimes makes his English incomprehensible to others.

After the 20-minute presentation, the class returns to the boardroom for the review process. Because there are only 20 minutes until lunch arrives, Eliana asks everyone to fill out a review form (see following page) individually (including Gordon, who does a self-assessment) so that the class can begin working in small groups after lunch.

Because there was some confusion about Gordon's job responsibilities, a few people find it difficult to write a two-sentence description of Gordon's work, as requested. Eliana suggests that those who are having trouble work in pairs so that they will be prepared for the group work that follows. After lunch, three or four small groups will try to work out a brief description together, pooling their ideas and helping each other with sentence construction.

Lunch arrives—the usual sandwich tray from the local supermarket, with drinks for all. Lately, the class has begun complaining about management's choice of lunch and Gordon is elected to talk to the manager about other take-out spots in the area. They agree that Chinese food or even pizza would be a welcome change, and even cheaper than the sandwich tray.

During the lunch break, Eliana slips out to the washroom located on the same floor, but outside the office. The only other space on this floor of a 12-storey highrise is occupied by a dentist's office. In the washroom, Eliana is stunned by the message written on a piece of paper taped to the mirror:

FLUSH THE F'ING TOILET. WHERE DO YOU PEOPLE COME FROM?
YOU DON'T KNOW YOU'RE SUPPOSED TO FLUSH?

Shaken, she reads it over silently several times. She knows the note is directed at course participants, the only workers on the floor who are members of visible minority groups and fit the "you people" category. She decides to pull the paper down and get the reaction of the class.

When she returns, everyone is chatting and finishing up lunch. She checks with them to make sure that there are only two offices on the floor, then relates what happened. She tapes up the note and people stare in silence. Eliana can only imagine how difficult this is for the Sri Lankan women, the two people from Mauritius, the Jamaican woman and the black Haitian man. Everyone else in the class could pass for "us" rather than "you people."

Eliana asks if anyone has ever encountered anything like this at work before. At first, there is no answer so she directs participants' attention to the note itself and asks, "Who might have written this?" and "Who was it intended for?"

The discussion begins slowly and hesitantly, not because of incomprehension but because class members are reluctant to approach this hurtful message. Answers are offered with a recognition that someone is labelling some class members different, unacceptable in this society and certainly not part of "us."

REVIEW OF TOUR

Presenter_____

COMMENTS ON PRESENTATION

Strong Points	*Needs Improvement*
Structure	Structure
Presentation (including language use)	Presentation (including language use)

Write a brief (two-sentence) description of this person's work:

Write the brief description that your group will present:

Jean, the Haitian man who is bilingual in French and English and has lived most of his life in Canada, says:

"Yeah, I've had that happen to me here on the telephone. I don't know what to say. I was talking to a lady long distance in Montreal who was receiving our mail. We just started talking a little bit and she told me how nice it was to talk to me. She liked my French—but you know she couldn't tell that I wasn't like her, that I was black. So, she starts telling me how unhappy she is that there are so many foreigners coming into Montreal, especially 'those kinds, you know, the Chinese and the blacks. It's nice to know you are one of us,' she says to me. Well, what do I say? I can't get into an argument with her on the phone so I just say 'yeah' and get off as fast as I can."

The class is silent for a short time letting the story sink in—a story that Jean has never told any of his colleagues. Eliana waits for another story but no one begins; in fact, she is surprised that Jean felt comfortable enough to tell this story because class members have not yet formed strong bonds and are still in the process of learning to trust one another.

She decides to pursue Jean's story and asks what responses might be possible in this situation. Although one person suggests that he interrupt the woman's comments by telling her he's black, most participants feel this response is just not possible in their work situation. Their supervisor frequently monitors their calls and would be displeased if Jean confronted a client, even one whose attitudes are racist. In addition, their calls are timed and unusually long conversations could be the subject of inquiry.

Jean adds:

"How do you really teach her anything on the phone in a short time? If I say something, she'll get angry or upset and probably refuse to be our client—then I'm the one on the hot seat, not her."

Another person suggests that Jean bring this up at a department meeting and see what his supervisor and colleagues think. This could be an opportunity to conduct some intensive, group problem-solving on an issue that affects many people in this multicultural office. People seem to feel that this is a good idea and encourage Jean to bring up the issue at the next meeting. He says he'll think about it.

Sensing that she has made the most of this opportunity, Eliana asks the class if class members would like to include the topic of racism and responding to racist remarks in future classes. Jean's story is rich in references to the makeup of Canadian society and to his role as a member of a visible minority group. Eliana suggests that they look critically at other situations they've encountered, read and discuss articles on the topic and follow up with their own written comments.

Participants seem to agree that they would like to include this in the course and Eliana says she'll put together some other concrete ideas for lessons to discuss with the class next week.

Len, the initiator of the course, uses this opportunity to suggest that he would like to start reading articles from newspapers and magazines, rather than focusing exclusively on company material. In fact, he says, he just read a good article on young Muslim women in Canada who are having difficulty with their strict parents. "And

Selima, you're Muslim, maybe you can give us more ideas about this." Selima smiles, a bit embarrassed but nods in acknowledgement. Len offers to bring in the piece and suggests that other class members take turns bringing in articles of interest.

By now, the time is almost up and people are starting to get restless. Because she recognizes that Len's suggestion offers a way to introduce the issue of cultural diversity, Eliana gladly accepts his offer to bring in the article. However, she suggests that a discussion of his proposal for involving other participants in finding readings of interest be put off until the next class. She can see that this issue will continue to unfold throughout the next few months. After class, Eliana thanks Len for the offer and asks him to bring in the article the next day so she can prepare some reading worksheets before the next class in two days.

On her way out, she stops to see the supervisor about Lorraine's absence and the current workload problem. Because of a change in systems, he says, the department just can't seem to make any headway. Eliana refers to the undertaking given by the supervisors and manager at the needs assessment meeting: participants would be covered during the two-hour class. He acknowledges this, but doesn't see a way around the problem for now. Because his own complaints haven't been effective in changing the situation, he suggests that Eliana speak to the manager.

Eliana sees the manager's secretary and books an appointment for a quick, 15-minute talk before the next class.

At home that night, she searches through some of her own books on diversity and anti-racism for teaching ideas. She remembers that Jan Gaston, in *Cultural Awareness Teaching Techniques*, develops a lesson on "country talks." This involves class members in making presentations about their country and culture in a social, political and historical context. Eliana thinks this might help promote understanding and tolerance, as well as offer another opportunity for making presentations. She decides to see how the article on Muslim women is received by the class and let the direction develop from there.

Books containing material on promoting cultural awareness are listed in the resources section of this book.

SEQUENCE 2

CLASS PROFILE

- Hospital workers: a total of 11 class members; eight women from housekeeping, two men and one woman from laundry.
- Course, which takes place at the end of the work day, is sponsored by management. Time is shared equally between the workers and the company.
- Classes are held in the boardroom. A chalkboard, flip chart, refreshments and space for storing supplies are provided by the company.
- Classes are held twice a week for $1\frac{1}{2}$ hours each time. Course will last three months.

- Native languages: Chinese, Polish, Tagalog, Portuguese.
- Range of ages: 34-55
- Levels of education in native country: Grades 2-6.
- Years in Canada: six months to 18 years.

LANGUAGE LEVELS AND NEEDS

Most of the people in the class are at a basic literacy level in English. Very little reading and writing is demanded on the job and what is required can be managed by everyone. Literacy is usually dealt with in class in a community context rather than a work context.

The oral interaction skills of the participants vary. One woman is just beyond the survival level in English, two or three speak English rather haltingly, and the rest are, for the most part, comprehensible, though their speech is marked by many grammatical and sociolinguistic errors. The hospital requested the course after some supervisors and patients complained about the inability of a few housekeepers to communicate (speak and listen) adequately. Requests and instructions had not been understood and therefore had not been acted upon. Most of the people in class recognize their need for improved listening and speaking skills, although the more fluent speakers specifically requested literacy work. If this three-month session is successful, the hospital is willing to continue classes and increase the hours if desired.

THE CLASSROOM

People start arriving five or 10 minutes early, some with their coffee from the cafeteria. Diana, the teacher, welcomes back Mr. Wong after his two-week absence and joins him for a brief chat about the illness that kept him from work. When everyone has taken their seats, Diana introduces the literacy work she has prepared for the day.

Katarzyna, one of the newer workers, and her friend are engaged in what appears to be an intense conversation in Polish. When Diana approaches them with the handouts, she inquires about problems. Katarzyna, who can make herself understood although with some difficulty, tells Diana that the head housekeeper just reprimanded her for working too slowly. Before getting the details, Diana asks the rest of the class to review their reading and writing homework in the usual manner (small groups correct their own work and then report any major problems).

Diana talks to Katarzyna for a few minutes and figures that the head housekeeper had probably said something like: "You don't have to spend so much time in the rooms. Either you work too slowly or you talk too much." Katarzyna felt unable to defend herself adequately and could only say that she was working as quickly as she could. This had not been satisfactory for either party and so the issue seemed unresolved. Diana asks Katarzyna if it would be all right to deal with the problem in class and she agrees. Because this issue goes to the heart of the hospital's motivation for initiating the course, Diana decides to set aside the lesson planned for the day.

After the small groups report on the homework and problems are cleared up, Diana takes up Katarzyna's problem. To place the problem in the larger context of responding to enquiries and reprimands, she asks the class who else has had similar problems either at work or elsewhere. One of the men comments on a misunderstanding about the weekend shift that had made his supervisor furious. Since the incident, he always confirms his schedule with the supervisor. With some help from her Chinese co-worker, Mrs. Li tells of the time she did not understand the nurse's instructions to clean one particular room first. Fortunately, there was no emergency involved and the nurse offered understanding and assistance rather than a reprimand.

By this point, Katarzyna no longer feels isolated by her experience or by her reaction and has gained the support of the class. For the last half hour, Diana suggests that they focus on Katarzyna's interactions with the head housekeeper. Briefly, they establish the background for the interaction:

What is the situation?
- Head housekeeper reprimanded Katarzyna for working too slowly and, indirectly, for talking too much to patients.

When and *Where*?
- At the end of the day.
- In the hallway.

Who	Job	Attitudes/Feelings	Relationship
Katarzyna	Housekeeper	Hectic day/short-staffed Problem at home this morning	Cool but workable
Barbara	Head housekeeper	Pressured/stress	Doesn't seem sociable

With these factors in mind, Diana sets up a role-play between herself as the head housekeeper and Katarzyna. She suggests that it be recorded and, after everyone agrees, the tape starts rolling.

Diana: Katarzyna, I'd like to talk to you for a minute.
Katarzyna: Yes.

Diana stops the tape and asks Katarzyna what her response means. Is it a question implying, What would you like to talk about? Or does she mean "okay," implying that she understands? Katarzyna indicates that it means she understands and motions to Diana to start again. This time she uses okay, but Diana thinks it sounds a bit abrupt, especially considering that the head housekeeper is "touchy" today. She asks the class how the reply sounded. "Surprised" and "scared" are the answers. Other women suggest replies with a different tone, more noticeably neutral. Mr. Wong suggests,

"Want see me now?" Katarzyna agrees and tries again, saying, "Do you want see me now?"

Once Katarzyna has been guided to notice her tone as well as the content of her reply, she begins to correct herself as the role-play moves on. Diana tries to keep the exchanges simple so the women with minimal speaking and listening skills won't lose interest. After a few more exchanges, Katarzyna is still unable to respond to the head housekeeper's reprimand—"You're too slow or you talk too much." Katarzyna can only say, "I can't work more fast."

At this point, Diana stops to explore the problem more deeply. "Do you feel hurried?" she asks Katarzyna. "Do you want to talk to the patients?"

With a little help from her Polish friend, Katarzyna explains that she finds it hard to leave a room when a patient is talking to her. "Why not explain this to the head housekeeper?" Diana asks. Katarzyna laughs and shrugs her shoulders.

When one woman suggests that she say, "I want leave but no can say to patient," Katarzyna offers this as a reply. José, taking the head housekeeper's role, says humorously, "Then go to English class!" With a good laugh, the tension is relieved. The role-play is reviewed once more and everyone agrees to practise "getting out of rooms" in the next class.

THE FOLLOW-UP CLASS

For the next class, Diana decided to make two short tapes simulating interactions between patients and housekeepers. She contacted two other housekeepers, both native English speakers, who enthusiastically offered their assistance. Diana explained the kind of language problem encountered and the housekeepers agreed to try the simulations. One even offered to involve a patient (with permission) but, with time at a premium, Diana decided to save this for another situation. In one of the simulations, the patient accepts the housekeeper's reason for leaving the room and, in the other, the interaction is not satisfactory and the patient is left abruptly.

Diana begins the class by replaying the role-play taped in the previous session. Laughing again at José's remark, the class recalls what their work is today—to practise talking to patients. The class breaks up into two groups to listen to the tapes Diana prepared ahead of time. Diana asks Mrs. Li to try working without her friend this time. Laughing but a bit nervous, Mrs. Li agrees to give it a try. Because Katarzyna is supportive and understanding of other learners, Diana makes sure that she is placed in Mrs. Li's group.

Each group listens to one of the tapes. The first time they listen for the general drift of the interaction—what's happening between the housekeeper and the patient. When they listen a second time, Diana asks them to identify the patient's specific requests ("You don't have to go yet?" and "You want to hear a good story?") and the responses of the housekeepers ("We're short-staffed today so I really have to go" and "I can't stay now."). Then she asks them to listen again, this time paying particular attention to the housekeeper's tone of voice and obvious indications of being willing or unwilling to listen to the patient.

The groups exchange tapes and repeat the steps of the analysis. The, Diana brings everyone together to compare their ideas and reactions. On the chalkboard, she notes examples of the kind of language used by the housekeepers to start and end the conversations and to indicate their attention while listening ("Oh really...," "Yes, I know...," etc.). She asks the class to suggest other possible options, which she records on the board, and they discuss their appropriateness.

After a short break for refreshments, the class divides into pairs to create some similar short role-plays. Following Diana's suggestions, some pairs choose to rework the unsatisfactory version they have just heard to bring it to a successful outcome, while others choose to explore different situations, picking up on the problems discussed in the previous class. Diana visits the pairs and asks two groups to tape their role-plays. One of then, which includes a humorous and successful conclusion, is transcribed here:

Patient: Want to hear a good story before you go?
Housekeeper: We're short-staffed today so I really have to go.
Patient: The story's funny. Make you a good laugh.
Housekeeper: Oh, tell my supervisor. She needs a good laugh!

The second role-play demonstrates another instance of a housekeeper's inability to respond. It concludes with the patient saying abruptly, "Get me the nurse."

At this point, Diana notices that the class has run a few minutes overtime. She calls a halt to the work and explains that the taped role-plays will be used in the next class. A few people ask to borrow the tapes to listen to over the weekend and, as well as listening, Diana encourages them to try taping new conversations with their families or coworkers.

While everyone is preparing to leave, Diana jots down a few ideas about how she'd like to use the class role-plays. By splitting the class, the more able speakers can analyse why the humorous tape is considered a successful interaction while she helps learners whose skills are more limited develop a repertoire of responses. She will take them through the exchange by labelling and writing each turn, thus allowing them enough time to think and practise without feeling pressured. Then, while the other group follows up on their literacy work, she will introduce the unpredictable element in a structured role play.

CHAPTER 8 # Assessment and Evaluation

T his chapter focuses on how ESL teachers can assess learners' progress and evaluate the success of the program. In most cases, we have used the term "assessment" to refer to the process of measuring the performance and progress of the learners, while "evaluation" refers to the process of measuring the overall success of the program. In this, the learners' progress is just one—very important—factor.

Because workplace courses involve many more relationships and more specific needs than most general ESL courses, learners' progress depends on a variety of factors: the level of sponsor support; the success of the negotiation process; the identification of learners' needs related to the workplace; and the materials used to meet these needs. Furthermore, any monitoring of learners' performance and progress must occur in the context of an overall evaluation of the entire program. This evaluation takes place not only at the end of the course, but also continuously throughout the course. In both instances, a number of participants is involved in each procedure:

Assessment of learners:

- The learners themselves (self-assessment).
- The teachers.
- The supervisor or union representative or both.

Evaluation of the program:

- The learners.
- The teachers.
- The sponsors.
- The educational institution.
- A committee of partners representing all the stakeholders.

Angela Gillis's article, "Evaluation: The Experience of One Hospital" (see Chapter 13), expands on the assessment theme by describing how a team approach can be used to evaluate workplace programs. This approach, which involves a variety of stakeholders in working co-operatively through the process of evaluating both the administrative and educational aspects of the program, is an excellent method of building understanding, rapport and support among the many people affected by workplace courses.

For information and thoughts on the role of formal testing in workplace courses, see Chapter 4.

CONTINUING ASSESSMENT AND EVALUATION

If we believe that designing a syllabus (see Chapter 5) is a dynamic process, then the classroom objectives we set and the language activities we develop are the result of the constant interplay between investigation, analysis and evaluation. Evaluation includes a continuous monitoring of both learners' progress and the success of the program. For example, daily class objectives can be set only by considering the learners' performance in each previous class as well as the constraints and potential of the overall program. A rigidly planned syllabus does not allow the flexibility needed to accommodate learners' needs and interests as they emerge. With a more flexible syllabus, we can plan for next week based partially on what's happened this week.

When evaluating the overall program, we probably need to consider whether our classroom objectives are appropriate in light of the particular workplace setting or whether the materials we develop are suitable for the level, interests and needs of the learners.

> In one non-unionized textile factory, management had always resisted workplace classes, fearing that they might be used directly or indirectly to promote unionization. Later, pressure from within the industry itself forced management to reconsider and offer the classes. This left the teacher in a difficult position. In planning every lesson, she had to consider management's reluctance to hold the classes at all. If supervisors overheard a particular lesson, how would they interpret it? In one class, unemployment insurance was the focus of language activities. The workers had requested this topic because many of them faced layoffs during slack times of the year. When management asked the teacher to justify her choice, she was able to turn the situation to her advantage.

Rather than defending her choice by citing workers' requests and the proven history of layoffs, she invited the supervisor to look over her lesson plan and materials. Her openness effectively deflated management's concern and established a degree of trust. Nevertheless, throughout the course, she had to take into account the management factor when determining what topics to cover in class and how deeply to go into them.

TECHNIQUES

Observation is the most flexible and readily available tool for conducting continuing assessment. As the learners work on each task, we can observe how well they listen, speak, read and write by asking ourselves questions like:

- Can they handle and produce more language than they did a few weeks ago?
- What kinds of tasks continue to present problems for certain learners?
- Are learners at the basic literacy level increasing their store of sight words?
- Are learners recognizing communication breakdowns and beginning to cope with them?

Our daily observation of learners' successes and difficulties create an emerging profile of each individual that can be documented informally in a variety of ways. A daily journal can be used to note comments about the learners' performance and behaviour. Or, to track a learner's development more consistently, try noting comments in individual files that have been prepared for each person in the class. We can also use the journal to record requests and suggestions from supervisors or stewards, questions that may have occurred to us, or "bright ideas" that we don't want to forget.

Making our own journal entries after every class also provides the necessary time for reflection, which ensures that our next class will build on the strengths of the previous class and provide extra support for the weaknesses observed. In terms of overall program evaluation, the reflections recorded in our journals are invaluable for reviewing where we've been and deciding where we want to go next.

When writing skills are the focus of a course, try keeping separate file folders for each learner. These writing portfolios are their property and contain all their written work—drafts as well as final products. For instance, their worksheets and LEA stories with comments from us and other readers can be kept in the files. At times, we can review the work and carry on a dialogue with the learner by writing to each other. Not only do the portfolios document learners' growth, but they also provide a reference that the learner can use to check spelling, vocabulary, sentence structure, and so on.

When oral work is the focus, audio tapes or videos can serve the same function as portfolios. Learners' language experience stories, their role-plays or their interviews with other class members can all be taped.

With control over a body of their own work, learners can then be guided to assess their own progress. Perhaps midway through the course, we can assist them in reviewing their work to date in order to build their awareness of what they can now do and what still needs improvement. This type of review and self-assessment can only be effective, however, if we have encouraged them to assess their own performance and that of others throughout the course.

How can we do this? Chapter 6 described activities in which learners worked with each other and the teacher to evaluate their performance. For example, learners can listen to the role-plays and dialogues of others and comment on their performance. When did communication break down? Who handled it well and why? They can read what others have written, looking for meaning and focusing on how well their peers were able to organize facts and events and get an idea across rather than on grammar and spelling. With small groups or individuals, we can work together to determine what the standards for performance might be.

Learners can also be guided to assess their own progress by reviewing their achievement at the end of each unit. If class objectives are linked to the performance of certain tasks, then learners can assess themselves by judging how well they can perform these tasks. For example, the form on the following page was used as part of a mid-course self-assessment in a class that focused on reading and writing.

The learners' assessment of their own performance and progress is part of the process of setting short- and long-term objectives. Do we agree with the learners' assessment of themselves? Do we have time to confer with them about it?

Having judged themselves, learners might then be able to look critically at the entire course. Basically, we want to determine whether they are satisfied with the topics covered and the activities used in class. If learners contributed to the process of setting objectives when the course began, then we could review these objectives together. Do we want to change them in light of progress that has been made, of new interests or of changes in the work situation?

If the sponsors were involved in setting the objectives, they can make a valuable contribution to the continuing processes of assessment and evaluation. Many teachers suggest not only informing them about topics covered in class each week but also actively involving them in creating opportunities for learners to use the language they have learned.

One teacher makes a practice of giving the supervisor a weekly review sheet every Monday. She asks him to look over the topics, the problem-solving activities and the language items covered during the previous week. He can then be more aware of the situations in the workplace where this language is used naturally. His comments on how well the learners are handling these language situations provide valuable feedback for the teacher and learners.

If sponsors play this kind of role in the process, they will naturally make evaluative comments throughout the course. In the process, they may find that their expectations change. For example, they may begin by saying, "Get them to read and understand their safety manuals." As the course evolves, however, this request may change to, "Help them learn to ask for an explanation when safety measures are not understood." Or, they may come around to the view that increasing learners' self-confidence is the

READING AND WRITING
SELF-ASSESSMENT

NAME

	EASILY	WITH SOME DIFFICULTY	WITH A LOT OF DIFFICULTY	NOT AT ALL
I can write the name of my job and the activities I do.				
I can write the types of safety hazards in my job.				
I can write the names of the pieces of safety equipment I use.				
I can write the name of my location and the locations of others.				
I can find important information in a bulletin from the union.				
I can find specific information in a newspaper article.				
I can find specific information in safety bulletins and articles.				
I know the procedure for certain safety practices; e.g., refusing to work in unsafe conditions.				

first step—or even the primary goal—of an entire course. If sponsors have been involved in monitoring the progress of the course, they will be able to make a fairer and more realistic evaluation at the end.

Supervisors of participants in an ESL program in the corporate sector filled out the form on the following page midway through a course that focused on speaking and listening skills.

FINAL ASSESSMENT AND EVALUATION

If the process of assessment and evaluation has occurred continuously throughout the course, completing the same process at the end of the course should hold no real surprises. Nevertheless, the final assessments and evaluation has much broader uses for all the stakeholders. The team approach that Angela Gillis recommends in Chapter 13 satisfies demands for accountability in regard to current and future financing, publicizes the program and encourages company-wide or community-wide involvement. If we see a final assessment of the learners as one component of the larger process of evaluating the overall program, then its role is integrated rather than highlighted.

Final evaluations give all the stakeholders the opportunity to review the original goals within the context of what has been achieved. The results can be used to improve the entire process of analysing needs, designing a syllabus, and developing materials for future courses at the same site or at other locations. Final evaluations can also affect negotiation procedures, in-service teacher training, the marketing of courses and other types of communication training beneficial to the sponsor. In addition, conducting a follow-up assessment and evaluation after six months can provide a further indication of the success of the program, the willingness of the supervisors to accept some responsibility for maintaining the gains of employees and a need for further language training.

FINAL ASSESSMENT OF LEARNERS

Self-Assessments

Learners, teachers and supervisors all have a role to play in a final assessment of progress. For learners, the process should highlight autonomy and the need to continue learning beyond the specific course.

They can begin by looking at what they accomplished during the course—at what they can do now that they couldn't when the course began. To encourage them to take responsibility for their own learning, invite them to assess their gains and then consider what they will do to continue improving their skills.

In an advanced business language course focusing on speaking and listening skills, for example, the participants devoted one entire class to developing their own self-assessment form. Because participating in meetings was one of their objectives, they used a meeting format for this class, discussing objectives, tasks and the

SUPERVISOR'S MID-TERM EVALUATION
OF ESL PROGRAM

Although we have completed only four weeks of our workplace ESL program, we would like to know whether you have noticed any positive effects on the course participants who report to you.

Check the column that best describes their progress. Fill in N/A if the language function does not apply to the staff of your department.

	SAME AS BEFORE	SOME IMPROVEMENT	CONSIDERABLE IMPROVEMENT
Talking to supervisors			
Talking to coworkers			
Using appropriate expressions on the telephone			
Giving information (on telephone and in person)			
Asking for information (on telephone and in person)			
Summarizing and relaying messages (in person or on telephone) without errors that impede comprehension			
Elaborating or offering reasons when asking permission			
Speaking English more confidently			
Using appropriate grammar, tone and intonation in daily speech			
Please add your concerns about particular staff in your department.			

Adapted from material provided by Brigid Kelso, Skills for Change, On-the-Job Training Program, Toronto.
Designed for the Multicultural Workplace Program, Continuing EducationDepartment, Board of Education for the City of Toronto, Ontario

performance level they wanted to achieve. The form they designed is shown on the following page.

If learners' oral skills are very basic, bilingual assistance will probably be needed to obtain the kind of information we are seeking. Learners can be encouraged to identify specific instances where communication, once blocked, is now possible.

> In one workplace setting, a kitchen worker noted the first time she had the courage to try to read a waiter's written order rather than relying on an oral order from the chef. She read the order correctly and carried out the entire process herself.

This focus on achievement could logically be followed up by talking about instances where communication still needs improvement.

Sponsor's Role

Final assessments should always incorporate the initial language needs identified by the sponsoring organization. If the course was initiated because hospital dietary workers could not read menus, for example, then an indication of their progress toward this target is necessary. For example, by the end of the course, some learners may feel comfortable reading and discussing the menus, though others may not have reached the same performance level.

This brings us to the sponsor's role in the final assessment of learners' progress. If our relationship with representatives of the sponsoring organization has been healthy, then frequent discussions over needs, objectives and assessment have probably taken place throughout the course. In these discussions, we and the sponsors move closer to achieving a common understanding of the goals that are worth pursuing and the criteria for success.

In many cases, sponsor(s) overestimate how much can be learned in the designated time. One sponsor, for example, requested that hotel housekeepers learn to read and write basic English in a 12-week course that met for two hours a week. Without continuing discussion of this objective, this sponsor would assess learners' progress on the basis of his initial expectation. Continuing communication with the sponsor(s) can help them develop more realistic expectations and provide guidance for a more relevant measure of success.

Critical Incident

One technique for helping sponsors judge progress is to identify a "critical incident." This technique helps supervisors identify specific incidents that cause problems. Working with the supervisors on a biweekly basis, teachers can help them keep track of these communication "incidents" to see what changes are taking place and if they face the same problems at the end of the course. We can turn the critical incident technique into a positive commentary by noting when supervisors express pleasure and surprise over improvements in communication. A comment from the restaurant

SELF- AND PEER ASSESSMENT—BUSINESS LANGUAGE COURSE

TASK	DESIRED PERFORMANCE	PERFORMANCE ATTAINED
Small talk		
■ Starting conversation	Friendly, comfortable, natural, with something interesting to say; able to close smoothly	
■ Reading body language	Judge others' body language accurately; know cultural differences; pick up right clues, give right signals	
■ Listening actively	Concentrate, ask questions, indicate understanding	
Meetings		
■ Participation	Take part actively, say what's on your mind	
■ Interrupting	Do it politely, have courage + assertiveness + language	
■ Giving up the floor	Have ability and openness to include others	
■ Holding the floor	Sound firm and knowledgeable	
Telephone talk		
■ Professionalism	Sound knowledgeable, clear, calm, cool, collected; able to engage in small talk	
■ Clarity	Word stress; speak up; no verbal fillers, not too fast; work on accent and pronunciation	
■ Effective call	Test caller's understanding; give step-by-step instructions; be clear, specific; avoid jargon	
■ Coming across effectively	Friendly, approachable, helpful, knowledgeable, patient, with good style and content	
Speech Mechanics		
■ Intonation	Vary intonation to sound alive, friendly; avoid rising intonation at end of sentences	
■ Word stress	Learn, practise	
■ Convincing	Be firm; use accurate intonation, eye contact	
■ Confidence	Eliminate verbal fillers	
■ Sounding natural	Be yourself; have humour in voice	
■ Fluency/accuracy	Forget about making errors; have confidence	
■ Knowledgeable	Expand vocabulary	
■ Using pitch effectively		
■ Eliminating verbal fillers		

Adapted from material provided by Valerie Hickey, Multicultural Workplace Program,
Continuing Education Department, Board of Education for the City of Toronto, Ontario.

hostess about how successfully a waiter handled a customer's complaint, for example, is really an observation that progress is being made. Or, in an office setting, a supervisor may report that an employee now calls him on the phone rather than dealing with him in person, which was the only way he could function at first.

These observations also reflect on the course as a whole and become a valuable tool in the final evaluation of the program.

FINAL EVALUATION

Because the ultimate use of any program evaluation is to make the next program better, final evaluations are the key to survival and success. Each of the stages of a workplace program can be evaluated for its effectiveness: the negotiations and needs analysis carried out to set up the course; the setting of overall objectives and, more specifically, designing a syllabus; the development of materials for use in class; the roles of teachers and learners in deciding on methodology; the role of communication and classroom interaction in language teaching; the relevance of the subject matter and the language to the workplace and the wider community; the assessment and evaluation procedures themselves; and the degree of preparation and readiness of all the participants to mount and teach such a course.

At each of these stages, the participants in a program have certain responsibilities to fulfil. Learners, teachers, sponsors and the educational institution can evaluate the success of each stage in light of their respective roles.

QUESTIONNAIRES AND INTERVIEWS

Questionnaires are probably the most common way of eliciting information for course evaluation. Questionnaires are much more successful if they are teamed with or followed up by a personal interview. Because the written form is static, we usually get only what we ask for. The interview can provide an opportunity for relating anecdotes that point to critical incidents and for giving explanations that would never be found in print. Supervisors may feel uncomfortable with written questions, may not be used to dealing with them or may have reading and writing problems themselves. In these cases, oral interviews based on points in the questionnaire are best.

Another drawback of questionnaires is that they often focus solely on language development. In interviews, other stages of the program, such as the negotiation process, the advertising and recruiting procedures, scheduling, etc., can be explored.

The final course evaluation form on pages 127-128 was used in an advanced business course that focused on writing. Participants filled in this form, which solicited their comments on course objectives, materials used, skills learned and benefits on and off the job.

The more general program evaluation form for managers and supervisors on pages 129-130 provides a good starting point for interviews. Using the questions as a guide, the interviewer can follow up with supplementary questions designed to elicit the kind of detailed responses that contribute to a thorough evaluation.

COURSE EVALUATION
BUSINESS LANGUAGE COURSE—GRAMMAR CLINIC

Please rate the following from 1 to 5 by checking the appropriate box.

	POOR 1	FAIR 2	GOOD 3	VERY GOOD 4	EXCELLENT 5
Overall rating of course (the course met my needs)					
Instructional style/approach to lessons					
Instructor's knowledge of subject					
Objectives were clearly stated					
Lessons were well-organized					
Material was relevant					
Material was stimulating					
Level of material was appropriate					

Do you feel you have improved in the following areas?

	YES	NO
Sentence structure		
Organization		
Grammar		
Spelling		
Punctuation		
Clear and concise writing		
Word choice		
Overall, do you feel your English writing skills have improved? NOT AT ALL ☐ SOMEWHAT ☐ VERY MUCH ☐		

Has this course helped you in your job?

_____

_____

How has this course helped you off the job?

_____

_____

Which part(s) of the course did you find particularly helpful or enjoyable?

_____

_____

Which areas would you have liked to spend more time on?

_____

_____

Which part(s) of the course, if any, were least helpful?

_____

_____

How could the course be changed or improved?

_____

_____

How satisfied were you with your participation in the course?

_____

Comment on the feedback given to you by the instructor.

_____

_____

Comment on the support given to your participation in the course.

_____

_____

Other comments?

_____

_____

_____

Adapted from material provided by Kristine Copkov and Florence Guy, Multicultural Workplace Program, Continuing Education Department, Board of Education for the City of Toronto, Ontario.

MULTICULTURAL WORKPLACE PROGRAM
WORKPLACE CLASSES—PROGRAM EVALUATION FOR MANAGERS AND SUPERVISORS

Please check the appropriate box.

	YES	NO	NOT SURE	NOT APPLICABLE
Is there an improvement in general conversation (work-related and social)?				
Has there been a change in morale and self-confidence among employees?				
Is there a better understanding of safety rules, policies, forms and other workplace documents?				
Has improvement of employees' skills affected their chances for promotion?				
Is there a noticeable improvement in reading comprehension?				
Have writing skills improved?				
Have there been fewer job-related misunderstandings?				
Is there a noticeable improvement in numerical efficiency?				
Has this program benefited the company?				
Has this program benefited the employees?				
Should the language classes be continued?				
Would other employees of your department benefit from language classes? How many? _____				

Please check the topic area in which employees could use some extra work:

- ■ Workplace vocabulary ☐
- ■ Following instructions ☐
- ■ Making simple requests ☐
- ■ Reading signs around the workplace ☐
- ■ Understanding policies and procedures ☐
- ■ Understanding WHMIS ☐
- ■ Having basic conversations ☐
- ■ Other ☐

_____

_____

_____

_____

_____

_____

We would like to encourage open communication with the trainer and company personnel. Please provide additional comments. Also, feel free to ask questions about the language classes.

_____

_____

_____

_____

_____

_____

Name (optional) _____

Company _____

Adapted with permission by Marni Johnson from "Workplace ESL and Literacy: A Business and Education Partnership" by Peggy Kinsey. In *Basic Skills for the Workplace* (M. Taylor, G. Lewe & J. Draper, Eds.). Toronto: Culture Concepts, 1991.

In one corporate setting, management brought together all the course participants in a focus group to evaluate all aspects of the program. Their discussion covered the following topics:

- Content of course.
- Improvements in their performance (why, how, barriers).
- Managing their time for study and work.
- Effectiveness of instructor.
- Program advertising, registration and continuation.

As mentioned previously, the assistance of a translator may be required to help learners whose English skills are at the basic level complete their evaluations. Often, it may be necessary to discuss the questions orally. However, basic level learners can also be asked to comment on the course objectives, activities and their own goals as the questionnaire on page 133, designed for a municipal program, shows.

STATISTICS

Industry statistics can also provide important evaluative information. Industries often judge the success of a program by assessing workers' performance on the job and work-related behaviour. Statistics relating to absentee rates, health and safety records, punctuality, staff turnover, promotions, raises, use of interpreters, etc. may be indicators of the success of a program. We should be cautious, however, about relying on these as measures of success because the most obvious and beneficial result of a course is very often an increase in the workers' confidence. Although this can be observed and acknowledged, it can't be measured in the same way as absentee rates.

Furthermore, statistics like this can be misleading unless they are fully explained and understood. They can be affected by many other factors. For example, despite improvements in communication and increased knowledge about safety, a company's health and safety record may remain poor because of unsafe conditions on the shop floor over which workers have little control. High absentee rates may have more to do with problems at home than with poor communication at the worksite. Achieving a promotion may depend not so much on a worker's facility with language as on the turnover of employees, the financial health of the industry, personality considerations or discrimination.

How far can workplace programs go in effecting major change in social and economic problem areas? Workplace literacy programs, for instance, are often promoted as the cure to many ills. In their contribution to *Basic Skills for the Workplace*, James Turk and Jean Unda clearly define the limitations of workplace programs as follows:

- Limited literacy in not a major cause of unemployment—lack of jobs is.
- Limited literacy is not a major cause of accidents and disease at work—unsafe working conditions and widespread use of toxic substances are.

- Limited literacy is not a principal cause of low productivity—inadequate capital investment, outdated technology and poor work organization are.
- Limited literacy does not account for Canadian industry's difficulties in international competition—foreign ownership, small research and development budgets, high interest rates and a high-priced dollar do.
- Limited literacy skills compound many problems but cause few. *The most important impact of improved literacy skills* would be to allow people to be better able to tackle these broader problems.

OUTCOMES, RECOMMENDATIONS AND WRITING THE REPORT

Evaluations provide an opportunity for all the stakeholders to review the roles they have played throughout the course. During this review, recommendations for further planning often emerge. For example, based on an evaluation of the strengths and weaknesses of the current program, recommendations could be made for subsequent programs at the same site or for new programs at different sites. In many cases, these recommendations redefine the roles of participants, clarifying the responsibilities of learners, teachers, sponsors and educational institutions.

For instance, when assessing the recruiting and advertising of a course, one co-ordinator of a program sponsored jointly by management and the union decided that more personalized publicity was needed. As a result, before the next session, the teachers and the co-ordinator held meetings with supervisors and shop stewards to explain the goals of the courses and enlist their support. Suggestions from these meetings led the teachers and the co-ordinator to attend employee health and safety meetings held in the evenings. Because of this pre-course field work, two additional classes were started at this particular worksite.

Every evaluation should include an examination of the effectiveness of each stage of a workplace program. For example, principles that have evolved from sound educational practice may need to be articulated by the teachers and the educational institution as a guide for the negotiation process. What are the minimum requirements for a successful workplace program? Or, because many of the teachers are new to the workplace setting or even to ESL, in-service training may be useful. In two separate programs, the teachers got together and, with the help of the co-ordinators, began organizing workshops for producing materials. This idea expanded when requests were made for paid leave to develop curriculum and, then, for developing a regular series of workshops on workplace teaching. Teachers often recognize the need for more specialized training in ESL literacy or in dealing with racism in the workplace, for instance.

Furthermore, recommendations for training may extend beyond the teachers and the learners in the language classes. Virginia Sauvé has suggested that workplace education "is more than a classroom activity. It is an intervention into the affairs of an organization."

EVALUATION OF COURSE

Name of course _____

Location of course _____

Sponsored by _____

1. Check the activities that you feel helped you in learning to read and write better.
   I learned a lot from:

   - ■ Reading the newspaper ☐
   - ■ Reading in a testing situation ☐
   - ■ Reading my job description ☐
   - ■ Reading the health and safety bill ☐
   - ■ Writing my own stories ☐
   - ■ Writing and reading forms ☐
     —banking ☐
     —minor accident forms ☐
     —application form ☐

2. Do you feel more confident about your reading and writing?
   A lot more ☐   A little more ☐   No ☐

3. Why did you sign up for the course in September?

   _____

4. Has the course helped you do that?
   Yes ☐   No ☐

5. Would you recommend this course to others?

   _____

6. Do you want to continue in January?
   Yes ☐   No ☐

7. If yes, do you want to work on...

   - ■ Speaking and listening ☐
   - ■ Reading and writing ☐

8. How can we make this course better?

   _____

   _____

   _____

Like the organizational needs assessment and the small scale needs analysis, a written evaluation report provides the opportunity to collect data, talk to employees in various departments, publicize the program and build support for improvements and for a commitment to life-long learning.

The written report itself can be structured in much the same way as the needs analysis report (see Chapter 4): simply substitute evaluation data and recommendations under the various headings. As with the needs analysis report, the best way to present the evaluation report is at a meeting of all stakeholders. In this setting, we can guide people through the report, answer questions and get feedback.

In summary, it's worth noting that the evaluation process may raise more questions than we can answer. We may find that, as teachers, our share of responsibility is ever-expanding. In this respect, evaluations highlight the varied nature of our job—we are negotiators, needs analysts, course designers, materials developers, teachers and evaluators. Evaluations show us where we have been and where we want to go. Progress may mean exploring the resources at our fingertips or turning to other models for inspiration. Evaluation provides the opportunity to reflect and, through reflection, to gain the insights we need to grow and improve.

When the cycle of workplace education—from the initial negotiations and needs assessment through the final evaluation—has been carried out co-operatively with the key stakeholders, everyone benefits. This excerpt is from a letter written by a supportive employer to Marni Johnson of the Etobicoke Board of Education's Multicultural Workplace Program. It captures the importance of this progressive process in transforming our working lives.

"While we could handle the technical aspects of the training and change required, we had no idea how to attack the more basic problems. Your expertise in planning, and providing the resources, was instrumental in getting us over this hurdle. The English in the Workplace, Understanding and Managing Diversity, and Team Building which you did (and are doing) has been a key factor in allowing us to gain the (quality) award.

"Perhaps in the long term, the most important results from this training are things that don't appear on the bottom line, or as a quality award: it is making (our company) a better place to work. Morale is up and people are communicating better than ever before. It is absolutely great to be able to really talk to workers who were virtually isolated from me a short time ago, and to see the pride they are taking in their accomplishments."

CHAPTER 9 # Conducting an Organizational Needs Assessment

by Sue (Waugh) Folinsbee

Although there is a great deal of literature on workplace literacy and basic skills, little material is available to help providers of workplace basic skills programs assess the needs of a workplace from an organizational perspective. As a result, this chapter outlines a process for conducting an organizational needs assessment as a first step toward determining whether a workplace basic skills program is desirable and whether other complementary activities are needed to reach organizational and employee goals. Leslie Elver, Barb Ward and I originally developed and expanded this process through the Multicultural Workplace Program at George Brown College in Toronto. It has evolved into a useful tool for determining basic skills issues within an organizational context.

ONAs are studies done within workplaces by outsiders to the organization to determine whether basic skills training is likely to address problems identified by the organization. If so, what kind of training would be suitable and for whom? If not, what other actions might be taken?

This chapter is written from the point of view of a provider offering services that address basic skills issues at the workplace to employers and unions. Possible service providers include labour organizations, community colleges, school boards, community literacy groups, community-based organizations and private consultants. They may offer a variety of services, including assessing needs, setting up workplace programs, providing trainers, training in-house or trades trainers, or training workers to be tutors. In addition to other services, they may also offer consultation around plain language.

WHAT IS AN ORGANIZATIONAL NEEDS ASSESSMENT?

UNDERLYING ASSUMPTIONS

The first premise of an organizational needs assessment is that issues relating to basic skills cannot be viewed in isolation from other critical workplace issues. Rather, they must be investigated within the context of the complex web of workplace and social systems.

A second premise is that strategies recommended to address basic skills issues need to recognize that they are inextricably linked to other workplace structures. Strategies that address workplace basic skills issues must do more than address narrowly defined skills in stand-alone basic skills programs. Innovative approaches, where basic skills issues are integrated into regular training, are needed. Moreover, an organizational development approach, in which organizations and unions and their structures are a focus for change in addressing basic skills issues and related issues, is necessary.

This is contrary to an approach that "blames the worker" and places the entire onus for change on individuals who are said to need to upgrade their basic skills. When the focus is solely on the shortcomings of individual workers, it is unlikely that all organizational, union or worker goals will be achieved.

PURPOSE OF THE ONA

The purpose of the ONA is to provide an overall analysis of the basic skills training needs from the perspective of the workplace and its members. In addition, it provides crucial information on:

- Critical factors that can affect workplace basic skills programs and their ability to achieve established goals and objectives.
- Other strategies besides stand-alone basic skills programs that need to be undertaken to address basic skills and related issues within an organization.

A DESCRIPTION

An ONA is a systematic approach to determining the basic skills training needs of a workplace within the context of the complex culture in which they occur. It involves input from workers, supervisors, managers and union leadership. It does not single out any employees, as the need for basic skills upgrading on the part of an individual is not a prerequisite for selection in the ONA. The ONA is a qualitative assessment that focuses on similarities and differences in perceptions of basic skills and other training and communication issues from the point of view of different workplace players. It provides a snapshot of the workplace at a specific point in time.

The ONA also examines the current organizational climate and culture as well as the oral and written communication systems of the workplace. This is crucial information for service providers who want to develop successful strategies for addressing workplace basic skills issues and strong partnerships with their clients. As a result of the ONA, clear courses of action can be recommended and priorities can be set. Moreover, it establishes a base for conducting task analyses or focusing on specific areas of need within the organization.

An ONA may be conducted by an outside service provider of workplace basic skills, the union or, internally, by the employer. However, employees may be more comfortable talking to their union representative or an outside party rather than their employer.

ONAs take many forms. In some cases, the service provider will be able to work with some kind of assessment that has already been carried out. In other cases, the union may be responsible for carrying out this kind of assessment by canvassing its members.

Although this chapter presents one way of conducting an ONA, there are many other creative ways of conducting this kind of assessment. A list of resources that provide other useful perspectives on ONAs and workplace basic skills is found in the bibliography. No matter how an ONA is conducted, it's important to remember that assessing basic skills within an organizational context is a crucial step in designing a strategy that addresses workplace literacy issues.

WHY CONDUCT AN ORGANIZATIONAL NEEDS ASSESSMENT?

BUILDING COMMITMENT, SUPPORT AND AWARENESS

The ONA enables service providers to gain support from and establish rapport with management, the union and employees within an organization without singling out employees or putting them at risk in any way. Because input is solicited from all levels of the workforce, an ONA encourages all stakeholders to buy into recommendations the service provider makes. This is more likely to happen when the expertise of all the players has been recognized through the consultative process. In addition, the ONA begins the process of raising awareness of workplace basic skills and establishing a respectful tone and use of language in talking about these issues. This is facilitated through the example set by the service provider and other partners.

PERCEPTION OF NEEDS ACCORDING TO ALL LEVELS OF THE WORKFORCE

Service providers cannot assume that the perceptions of the organization's contact person(s) about the basic skills issues will necessarily reflect those of the workforce and its stakeholders. Often, they do not; or they present only a partial picture. Take for example, this situation:

> The personnel director of a hotel called in the service provider to set up a workplace basic skills program for the hotel's multilingual, culturally diverse workforce. According to the director, a large number of employees wanted to get ahead but couldn't because of their written and oral communication skills.

He stated that at least 70 employees were anxious to attend a workplace program. The ONA showed that, although several employees were interested in a program, they didn't fall within the target group identified initially by the director. In fact, there was little interest from the departments identified at first. In addition, several other pressing issues were identified, such as the need for managers and supervisors to develop new skills in communicating with the multicultural work force.

OTHER CRITICAL FACTORS

The ONA establishes the real need for a workplace basic skills program within the context of an organization and the critical factors that are at play within it. These critical factors may suggest other strategies and activities that should be implemented along with a workplace basic skills training program. In rare cases, it pinpoints hidden agendas that have not been disclosed by management and that would jeopardize both the success of a workplace basic skills program and the position of the service provider and employees attending the program.

The following example illustrates how these critical factors might be at play:

In a manufacturing company, management wished to set up workplace basic skills programs to placate discontented workers and improve the morale of the workplace. During the course of the ONA, the writer discovered that the workers were discouraged, their input was never solicited and there were production problems because of antiquated machinery that was always breaking down. The level of discontent was so high that workers were divided in a struggle to organize the workplace. This fact was not presented in any of the initial meetings with management. By the time the ONA was concluded, it was apparent that a workplace basic skills intervention would have to be postponed until other issues at the workplace had been resolved satisfactorily.

MAPPING THE WORKPLACE CULTURE

Every organization has its own corporate culture with an overall philosophy, values, beliefs and codes of expected behaviour. The ONA helps the service provider map this workplace culture. This is critical information in assessing how to work successfully with an organization and address its needs. For example, an organization that considers itself to have a flat structure in which front-line workers appear first on the organizational chart and everyone is considered equal will need to be approached differently from one that has a well-established, top-down structure. Interactions in a unionized workplace will be very different from those in a non-unionized workplace. In a unionized workplace, there will be two equal partners instead of one.

The way in which a service provider communicates and establishes a strategy for developing a working relationship and partnership with an organization will depend very much on the culture of the workplace. Consider the following two different workplace cultures:

In a medium-sized manufacturing organization, open communication was encouraged and ideas from front-line workers were solicited on a regular basis. The organizational chart showed the front-line workers at the top of the chart as the company's most important asset, with the general manager appearing last. In addition, the employees, including the general manager, wore jeans and T-shirts to reflect the company philosophy of equality, which was espoused by the organization in its mission statement. As a result, the service provider found she had easy access to various individuals within the organization and that they were free and open in providing written and other information she needed. She was told that she could contact several key personnel directly, without going through the contact person each time.

A large trust company with a hierarchical structure and formal communication procedures provided a very different experience. Before the provider could talk to anyone, approval had to be granted by a number of people. Similarly, when the provider asked for company print material, approval had to be granted by several senior managers. In addition, she was required to sign a letter stating that she would not divulge the contents of any of the materials. No communication could occur between any employees and the service provider without the intervention of the company contact person. It took a great deal of lead time to get things done in this organization.

These two scenarios indicate that no two workplace cultures are the same and that the service provider needs to have a good grasp of the workplace culture to work effectively with an organization. The ONA enables the service provider to determine the organizational climate at the time and to become aware of external issues, such as a shrinking labour pool or increased competition, that may be affecting a particular industry or company.

THE ONA REPORT—BACKUP SUPPORT AND MARKETING TOOL

The ONA provides backup and support when the organization questions training and other recommendations made by the service provider. It places workplace basic skills in the context of other organizational strategies that need to be implemented along with basic skills programs to achieve organizational and employee goals. It helps organizations set priorities for training and other issues.

An ONA also helps the service provider clarify what can and cannot be accomplished through a workplace basic skills intervention. A workplace basic skills intervention refers to both training and other organizational development strategies that are undertaken to address issues relating to workplace basic skills.

Finally, the ONA report can be used as a marketing tool to convince employers and unions that they should invest time and money in basic skills training and other activities that address critical workplace issues and needs identified by employees.

THE RELATIONSHIP OF THE ONA TO OTHER FORMS OF ASSESSMENT

Literacy task analysis and individual assessments are not a substitute for an ONA. The ONA does not intentionally focus on specific jobs or individuals who might benefit from a workplace basic skills program. Rather, it provides an overall picture of the workplace and sets the context in which both the assessment of individual needs and literacy task analysis can logically proceed.

The areas within an organization that may subsequently require a literacy task analysis should be clearly identified in the ONA. In *Basic Skills Training—A Launchpad for Success in the Workplace*, Maurice Taylor and Glenda Lewe identify literacy task analysis as the "defining of the literacy elements to do specific jobs." Although there are many ways to perform a literacy task analysis, the focus should be on the literacy elements involved in a particular task, rather than on the "skills deficiencies" of a particular worker.

Individual assessments for employees who will be attending workplace programs should be custom-designed for the workplace and non-threatening. In addition, they should take into consideration the individual aspirations and interests of the employees. For example, a personal interview can focus on the specific needs, interests, fears and concerns of employees. In addition, tasks built around basic skills requirements designed from workplace materials can simulate what the employees do on the job and assess their skill level in completing these tasks. The need for confidentiality cannot be stressed enough. These results must be kept confidential by the service provider.

The needs assessment strategy used will depend on the size, nature and needs of a particular workplace. Information from a combination of literacy task analysis, individual assessments and the ONA will become the basis for developing learning objectives. In using these three sources of information, a service provider can ensure that the objectives and content of workplace basic skills programs balance the needs of all the stakeholders in the workplace—program participants, management and the union.

SITUATING THE ONA

The chart on the following page clearly shows where the ONA fits into the overall process of implementing a workplace basic skills intervention.

Initial Contact Interview

The initial contact interview with a client actually provides the basis for determining an ONA strategy. In addition to listening carefully to the basic skills and other communication needs identified by the client, the provider needs to probe other important areas, such as:

- The composition of the work force (gender, race, ethnicity, age).
- Technological and other changes that have taken place at the workplace.

AN OVERVIEW OF THE STEPS IN SETTING UP
A WORKPLACE BASIC SKILLS INITIATIVE

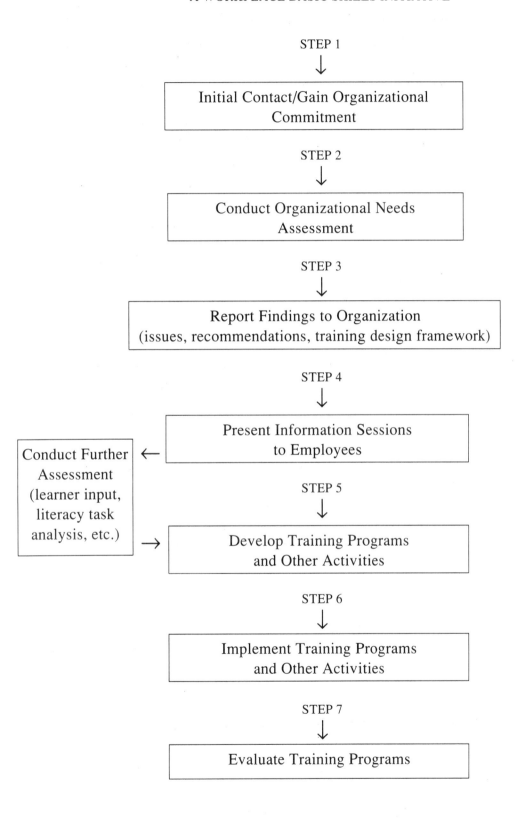

STEP 1
↓

Initial Contact/Gain Organizational
Commitment

STEP 2
↓

Conduct Organizational Needs
Assessment

STEP 3
↓

Report Findings to Organization
(issues, recommendations, training design framework)

STEP 4
↓

Present Information Sessions
to Employees

Conduct Further
Assessment
(learner input,
literacy task
analysis, etc.)   ←

STEP 5
↓

Develop Training Programs
and Other Activities

STEP 6
↓

Implement Training Programs
and Other Activities

STEP 7
↓

Evaluate Training Programs

- Types of jobs performed.
- Number of shifts and duration.
- Peak periods.
- Shutdowns.
- Turnover, layoffs.

AN OVERVIEW OF THE STEPS

The following chart outlines the process involved in conducting an ONA. It is an expansion of Step 2 of the previous chart, "An Overview of the Steps in Setting Up a Workplace Basic Skills Initiative."

ORGANIZATIONAL NEEDS ASSESSMENT PROCESS

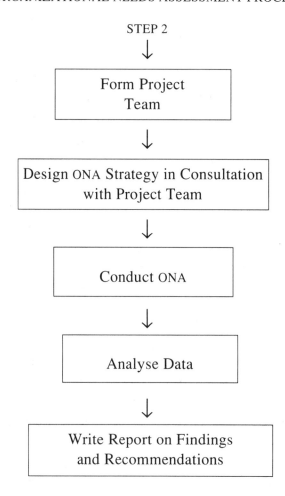

FORM PROJECT TEAM

The success of a workplace basic skills intervention depends on the strength of the partnership that has been developed among the service provider, the employer and the union (if there is a union). In this partnership, service providers must be aware of the need for flexibility in working with organizations on their own terms. In determining the expectations of key members of the project team, the time that employees can devote to the undertaking must be considered. It is wise to be wary of an organization that does not want or expect to have any input and expects service providers to do everything on their own.

Once the organization and union have agreed to invite the service provider to conduct an organizational needs assessment, a project team should be formed. Its purpose is to advise and assist in the process of conducting the ONA and implementing subsequent recommendations.

Ideally, the project team should include one senior manager, one union representative, one or two supervisors and one or two employees. Team members should be chosen by management and the union on the basis of their commitment to addressing workplace skills, their ability to provide useful information and feedback on all aspects of the process and the fact that they are respected by their coworkers.

The members of a project team, if chosen carefully, can help build support for and commitment to the ONA and subsequent steps in the process of implementing a workplace basic skills intervention. In many cases, there may be education or other committees already in place from which the project team can be drawn.

These, of course, are ideal circumstances. In many cases, especially in small companies, it is not possible to have a project team. In this case, the service provider may work with a company representative alone or, in unionized workplaces, with both a company and union representative.

DESIGN ONA IN CONSULTATION WITH PROJECT TEAM

Participants

Experience shows that surveying approximately 10 per cent of the workforce in the ONA provides an excellent, holistic picture of the needs of the organization. In large organizations where it is not feasible or cost-effective to concentrate on the entire organization at one time, specific departments may be targeted. On the other hand, in very small companies, it may be advisable to survey all employees.

This aspect of the ONA will need to be decided on with the project team or key management and union contacts. A good guideline to follow in large organizations is to start small and successfully with pilot projects in one or two departments. After successful projects are completed, basic skills issues in other areas of the organization may be addressed.

Participants in the ONA should reflect a representative sample of the various jobs, positions and shifts, as well as the gender, race and ethnicity of the workforce. The project team can recommend participants for the ONA, but participation must be voluntary. In cases where a high level of need in certain areas of an organization has been unanimously identified by the project team, the ONA may focus on a larger percentage of workers, supervisors and managers from these areas. However, front-line workers selected for the ONA should not be employees perceived as "needing" a workplace basic skills program. Some employees selected for the ONA may eventually attend a program, but their basic skills needs should not be the central reason for their participation in the ONA. If an organization has a company nurse, doctor or employee assistance program counsellor, they should be interviewed.

Areas to Probe

Because the ONA should identify similarities and differences in the perceptions of employees regarding workplace issues and needs, the same questions should be asked of all participants. Depending on the participants, however, these questions may be worded differently. The project team will be able to advise on the wording of questions. One point to remember is that, in order to receive the richest information and cut down on interviewer bias, the questions should be open-ended.

Key areas to probe with participants in the ONA and from which to develop questions include:

- Changes they have seen at the workplace and the impact of these changes.
- Their job and what it includes.
- Who they communicate with and what they communicate about.
- Impact of cultural, racial and linguistic diversity.
- Whether they work in a team or alone.
- What reading, writing and mathematics employees use to do their jobs (management and union representatives would be asked to comment on their own jobs as well the jobs of other workers).
- Where there might be difficulties in these areas.
- What kind of training in these areas might be useful for employees in general.
- Other training needs.
- If training programs in these areas were offered to employees, what exactly they should include.
- What training and orientation they (and their employees or members) received when they started working for the company.
- How people get promoted.
- How communication could be improved at the workplace.

Methodology

Confidential, face-to-face interviews and focus groups provide the best methods of conducting an ONA. Interviews that promise confidentiality and anonymity can successfully tap the perceptions of the workforce. They should usually last no longer than half an hour and be conducted in a private place. Focus groups work most effectively with supervisors and managers. They are useful in identifying the similarities and differences in perceptions of needs and issues. At the same time, a byproduct of the focus group may be heightened awareness of basic skills issues. It is generally not a good idea to mix workers and supervisors in a focus group. Workers may be reluctant to state what is really on their minds if their supervisor is there to hear it. Focus groups may last as long as two or more hours.

Questionnaires are not a recommended tool for the ONA for many reasons. First, there is a built-in assumption that employees will have the skills to complete the questionnaire and, second, that they will feel comfortable putting their opinions in writing. In addition, a questionnaire does not allow for further probing of key points that may be raised.

Pilot Testing the Instrument

Members of the project team can provide valuable feedback on questions for interviews and focus groups by going through the process themselves. Not only can they provide important feedback on the suitability of the questions but, through the pilot testing, they can also provide another source of input for the ONA.

Other Components

A workplace tour is an essential component of the ONA. This may occur during the initial contact interview or during a subsequent meeting. Bulletin boards, workplace signs and slogans, company newsletters and posters can provide useful information on both the workplace culture and the work-related reading required of employees.

A sampling of job-specific reading material can be examined by the service provider to determine whether it is appropriately geared to the needs and skill levels of the workforce. This will be useful at the literacy task analysis stage as well. Customer complaint records, end-of-shift reports, test results and participants' evaluations from other training programs can also provide useful insights into the skill levels of the workforce and the need for a workplace basic skills intervention. Again, the combination of methods used in the ONA will depend on the organization's resources, the culture of the workplace, size of the organization, type of industry and employee comfort level.

Informing Workforce about the ONA

The service provider, in consultation with the project team, will need to develop a way of informing the entire workforce about the ONA, its purpose and how participants have been selected. This is an important step. If the entire workforce is not informed about what is going on, rumours begin and mistrust on the part of employees as to the real purpose of the ONA and its ramifications will build rapidly. The workforce can be informed of the ONA through a joint management-union memorandum or through personal contact with members of the project team.

Conducting the ONA

Once the ONA strategy has been developed and logistics for implementing it determined, the key to success is the ability of the person conducting the assessment to develop rapport and trust with selected participants in a short period.

The ethnographic interview is an important technique that can be used successfully in both the ONA and individual assessment to understand the culture of the workplace and the people in it. In *The Ethnographic Interview*, James Spradley points out that, in this situation, researchers become students in that they learn from the people they interact with as they set aside their own biases and assumptions to interpret what is going on.

The same principles can be applied when a service provider conducts an ONA. This means consciously starting the assessment from ignorance as much as possible. It also means using the language of the interviewees when probing with further questions and avoiding the temptation to skip questions because we think we know the answer already. Active listening, in which understanding is checked frequently, ensures that the service provider and employee are on common ground and that the assessor has correctly interpreted the input of the respondent. Open-ended questions are much more successful in eliciting information from the assessment than closed questions.

Other important factors to remember when conducting the ONA are, first, that a clear explanation of the purpose of the ONA must be given at the beginning of an interview or focus group; second, that respondents are assured of confidentiality; and, last, that they understand that they are under no obligation to answer any questions about which they feel uncomfortable. Interviews and focus groups should be conducted in a private, quiet space. Service providers must be prepared to be flexible and ready to deal with on-the-spot situations during the ONA process.

Establishing rapport with participants in the ONA is paramount. Sometimes this will be difficult, especially in the case of supervisors or senior managers who are not yet convinced that there is a need to address basic skills. Allowing people time to get their viewpoint and real concerns across will go a long way toward building bridges for the future. Moreover, the concerns and needs expressed may not be the same as those of the service providers. Therefore, it is important to encourage participants in the ONA to express their opinions and concerns.

Because their opinions may never have been solicited before, some employees will be overwhelmed at being asked about issues related to the workplace. The job of the service provider is to put these respondents at ease so they feel comfortable with the process. Other employees may try to get a service provider to agree with their opinions or take sides on workplace issues. The provider's task is to gain an understanding of the workplace and its issues and needs while remaining impartial.

In addition, some respondents may voice opinions that are in direct conflict with what the service provider believes to be true. Some of these opinions may be perceived as offensive. It must be stressed that the ONA process is not a tool for educating respondents. Furthermore, management may inquire about what certain employees said during the ONA. This situation must be handled tactfully. Referring back to the agreement about the confidentiality of the results and assuring management that major issues will be included in the written report usually defuses this kind of situation.

Analyse Data

Once all the components of the ONA are complete, the data collected must be analysed and categorized according to the issues participants identified, as well as other findings. A framework for analysing the data collected during the ONA has been adapted from one presented by Leslie Elver, Tara Goldstein, Joan McDonald and Julie Reid in *Improving Intercultural Communication in the Workplace: An Approach to Needs Assessment*. This framework includes basic skills issues, other training issues and structural issues. Basic skills issues may include reading, writing, problem-solving and oral communication skills. These needs may apply to first or second language speakers. Numeracy upgrading may also be included under basic skills. Other training issues might include technical issues, health and safety issues, management issues, plain language and on-the-job training.

In multicultural workplaces, there may be a need for intercultural communication and race relations training or training in "managing diversity." Non-training issues form the third major category. Non-training issues might include needs related to promotion practices, orientation programs, performance appraisals, communication channels, employment equity, readability of print material, and management style. The ONA report can be done in chart or narrative form. A good strategy is to find the format favoured by the organization in reports of its own.

Write Report with Recommendations and Macro Program Outlines

It is important to present the findings of the ONA in a clear, consistent fashion in language that the client can understand. The report should include:

- An introduction that includes background information leading up to the ONA, and the ONA strategy.
- A summary of the issues identified during the ONA process, with examples.
- Recommendations including overall workplace program designs, other organizational strategies and a procedure for conducting further assessment, such as a literacy task analysis, presenting programs to employees and conducting individual assessments.
- A breakdown of costs.
- A conclusion.

It's a good idea to walk the contact person(s) through the report before presenting it to the project team. It is not advisable to simply send a completed report to an organization without this personal walk-through. This process helps identify ideas that are not expressed clearly or information that may be taken out of context so that they can be adjusted. Ideas that have been presented can be elaborated on. The project team's feedback on the report should serve as a validation of the findings in the ONA.

CONCLUDING COMMENTS

When service providers go into the workplace, ways of doing things that have worked well in their own institutions may not be appropriate. For example, an intake model used in continuing education departments of educational institutions in which participants are "signed up" for courses without an ONA is not advisable; neither are programs that focus only on assessing the personal and community needs of employees. The needs of the organization as an entity made up of many different players must be assessed. An ONA gives direction to recommendations that the service provider makes.

Service providers must be flexible in working within organizational parameters. For example, to ensure that a sampling of employees on all shifts is included in the ONA may mean surveying employees in the early hours of the morning or late at night. Similarly, the service provider needs to work within the time constraints of the project team and employees. As visitors to the workplace, service providers must get to know each organization on its own terms. Workplaces must be approached as if we are learning a "new culture." Biases, assumptions and personal agendas must be set aside when conducting an ONA. The "real stories" told in the words of ONA participants must be heard.

Service providers also need to be prepared to deal tactfully with unexpected, on-the-spot situations. Some examples of these situations have already been described. The most common situation service providers have to deal with occurs when ONA participants are not ready to divulge much information for a variety of reasons. No one should be obliged to participate in the ONA or answer questions that cause discomfort. Other situations require the service provider to show empathy, practise impartiality and preserve confidentiality.

Because organizations differ, each must be approached creatively. This may mean developing and implementing different ONA strategies depending on the nature of the workplace situation and its players. A service provider must be enterprising and innovative—without compromising the ONA process. When employees representing different areas and positions in the organization have been actively involved in developing and implementing the ONA, the process is more successful. When employees are consulted, they tend to feel ownership of the process.

An effective ONA can provide a solid, positive base from which to build a successful workplace basic skills intervention. Moreover, the ONA begins the process of establishing rapport and building trust among the service provider, its partners and employees. As a result of the ONA, subsequent steps in implementing a workplace basic skills intervention can be accomplished more accurately and smoothly.

CHAPTER 10

Responding to Racism in Workplace ESL

by Kathleen Flanagan

This chapter explores the impact of racism on workplace language programs: the forms that racism takes in this setting; the effects it has on instructor-to-learner and learner-to-learner interactions; the responses that are available to ESL teachers; and the conditions that contribute to challenging racism.

The concerns raised, perspectives offered and strategies suggested are based on a series of interviews with seven ESL teachers who have identified anti-racism education as a key component of their language classes.

RACISM AND ESL

Many ESL teachers who teach in the workplace recognize that issues of race inhabit their classrooms. A number of interconnected factors combine to create this situation. The ESL curriculum, for example, is likely to present aspects of Canadian history and culture with racial implications, without discussing alternative points of view. Or, in learner-centred education, which uses students' identities and experiences as the starting point, experiences of racist treatment may be raised in classroom discussions.

Some educators suggest that education plays a role in maintaining and justifying racial inequities. In *Experience, Research, Social Change: Methods from the Margins*, Sandra Kirby and Kate McKenna take this suggestion farther, arguing that knowledge is constructed within a context of power relations—largely determined by class, gender and race—that are a significant factor in creating and teaching knowledge. In addition, the process of learning in a formalized setting often involves an unacknowledged power relationship between teacher and learner with race, class, and gender implications.

From this point of view, all learning contexts are layered with racial meaning. ESL classes are particularized learning arenas with additional racial implications. Language itself conveys societal attitudes and ideas, including deeply embedded racial biases and stereotypes, which may be incompatible with the needs or beliefs of the learners.

Furthermore, the need to learn one of Canada's two official languages creates a situation that reveals veiled social contradictions. Examples of these contradictions abound. Canada's current policy of multiculturalism, for example, overlays the historic reality of a dominant monoculture based on British traditions that fostered cultural and linguistic assimilation, oppression of minorities, and racist immigration policies. The official commitment to racial and gender equality diverges from the widely acknowledged reality of systemic racism and sexism. The ideal of equal opportunity for all Canadian citizens is contradicted by the economic necessity for a wealthy society to have an oppressed underclass.

The dynamics of race relations that routinely affect the educational process as a whole and ESL classes in particular are amplified in language classes that are located in the workplace. Employment is one of the main areas in which racial discrimination is practised and experienced: this is apparent in biased hiring practices and promotion opportunities, cross-cultural misunderstandings, racial harassment, and exclusionary behaviour.

Jobs, which are intrinsically linked to security, income level, self-esteem, and the ability to construct a satisfying, meaningful and planned life, are extremely important in the lives of most people. According to an article by Mary Ellen Belfiore in *TESL Talk*, job-related concerns are the most common reason students cite for enrolling in ESL classes, particularly during difficult economic times when plant closures and downsizing are frequent occurrences.

These concerns are well-founded. In another article in *TESL Talk*, Tara Goldstein pointed out that garment and textile companies in Ontario, which employ large numbers of immigrant workers, laid off one-third of their workers between 1988 and 1990. Goldstein also notes that, according to an article that appeared in the *Toronto Star* in September 1991, 94 per cent of Toronto's sewing machine operators were born outside Canada.

Thus, several conditions intersect in workplace ESL classes to make race issues particularly significant:

■ ESL classes reflect the systemic racism embedded in society and the educational process.

■ The gap between the official ideals of equality and opportunity and the reality experienced by many non-white immigrants becomes more visible in an ESL setting in which the study of Canadian history, culture, language and laws may be included in formal or informal curriculums.

- Employment, an important concern to most people but particularly to immigrants who may lack access to the support networks available to non-immigrants, is a key area of racial discrimination. As a result, workplace language classes are likely to be affected by job-related racism.

instructors not trained in racial issues

Although there is no doubt that race issues reverberate in workplace ESL classes, instructors are not required to take anti-racism training, are not always able to recognize the issues, and may, because of this lack of knowledge, be unconscious and unwilling perpetrators of racism. Because ESL teachers often work independently in part-time and temporary situations, there are few opportunities to participate in formal professional development sessions or discuss race issues with other ESL teachers or anti-racism activists.

The purpose go to ch 10

The purpose of this chapter is to help workplace ESL teachers formulate a framework for analysing racism, reflect on their own personal reactions to the issue, and develop a personal position from which to challenge it.

THE INTERVIEWS

How does racism affect workplace ESL programs and how should instructors respond?

This question was put to seven experienced ESL instructors who actively promote anti-racism responses and strategies in their work. They were:

findings: 7 ESL instructors

- Tara Goldstein, University of Toronto
- Karen Lynn, Humber College
- Joan McDonald, McDonald Communications Consultants
- Simin Meshiginnafas, Sheridan College
- Kevin Moloney, ESL Instructor
- Winnie Ng, ESL Workplace Instructor
- Olga Reis, Metro Labour Education and Skills Training Centre

The interviews, which were conducted individually throughout February and March 1994, were taped and transcribed. The informants were chosen on the basis of several criteria:

- All have extensive ESL experience, ranging from 10 to 20 years. All have taught workplace ESL classes. Their work has involved close contact with other ESL instructors, either as supervisors or as colleagues working in a shared work environment. This contact has given them opportunities to discuss and reflect on their professional ideals, aspirations and activities.
- All have a special interest and involvement in promoting strategies that combat racism, both within and outside an ESL context.

- Most, though not all, of the informants identify themselves by their individual ethnic and racial origins, which include Iranian, Portuguese, Jewish, Chinese, and Irish identities. Two of the seven identify themselves as non-whites. Some are Canadian-born; several are immigrants or the children of immigrants. It was clear throughout the interviews that these diverse ethnic and racial identities have deep personal significance to the individuals and affect their delivery of language-training services.
- Within the anti-racist ESL context, the perspectives of the informants span a broad spectrum of opinions and approaches, reflecting their own socio-economic background, race, ethnicity, gender, age, life experiences, personal values, priorities, and world-views.

Using an open-ended, loosely structured approach, the interviews focused on the issue of racism within workplace ESL programs. Drawing on their own experiences, the informants were encouraged to describe the forms, functions, and effects of individual and systemic racism in this setting. They were also asked to delineate possible responses to, as well as strategies for combatting, manifestations of racism. A distinction was made between responses—immediate, spontaneous (although not necessarily unplanned) reactions to classroom-generated displays of racism—and strategies and tactics—anti-racist exercises and teaching approaches that are incorporated into the prepared curriculum. The instructors were asked to describe both effective and ineffective responses and strategies.

An additional aspect of the interviews revolved around discussions about the structural conditions that enable a productive examination and repudiation of racism. The instructors were encouraged to express their general thoughts and opinions, as well as specific, detailed suggestions.

All the informants showed themselves to be strong, personable, committed and reflective anti-racist ESL educators who agreed on three essential aspects of the discussion:

- Racism exists in ESL programs in a variety of forms.
- ESL teachers must choose to accept or challenge white-skin privilege (a "neutral" position indicates acceptance).
- Their choices must be supported by a consciously reasoned and articulated anti-racist plan of action that is developed and implemented with non-white input.

The informants also had clear and substantive differences of opinion and emphasis. These differences are valuable and useful because they add a multi-dimensional quality to the discussions by presenting the issues from a variety of perspectives, all of them shaped by considerations related to socio-economic background, race, gender and personal considerations. It is hoped that the different viewpoints expressed by the informants can provide ESL instructors who teach in the workplace with multiple access points to the issues.

WHOSE NEEDS?

Several of the instructors raised questions about the process of assessing the language needs of the learners. Whose needs are met by teaching English in the workplace? How are these needs identified? How are they understood? These questions were considered important. Most of the informants agreed that the goals for the language program defined by workplace owners and managers may be different from those defined by the learners.

note

> *Interview 2*: One area is the whole implementation of the program in the workplace. Who decides that a program is coming in? Who gets selected to participate in the program? What purposes does it serve? If it's a management-driven type of program, the agenda could be very different from a more worker-oriented, a more labour-oriented program. The difference in agenda would manifest itself in terms of the content of the instruction, who teaches, and the follow-up. Whose agenda does it serve? Whose needs, whose immediate needs, are being met in the classroom? I think workers go to the program with different expectations from management. Management might simply want workers to become more obedient.

> *Interview 6*: Part of what we do in ESL is because we want to make people good consumers and good workers. So it's all about how to respond to orders from a supervisor, rather than how to challenge orders from a supervisor. There is this kind of ideology that still dominates ESL, which is, you know, good citizen, good consumer, good worker. I've gone into a workplace and I've said, "Let's do something about work here," and the students say, "Aw, we know all about work language. He (the boss) says, 'Do this, do that,' and we do it. We want to know how to speak to our children's friends, how to speak to our doctor."

> *Interview 4*: When we design our needs assessments, the kinds of questions we ask are already narrow because we're assuming that people need English for certain purposes. For example, not all workers need to speak English at work. As well, a lot of people have a vested interest in the learners' learning something, you know. I think we make assumptions about what kinds of needs people have. There is often a conflict over different people's needs. Management may want the workers to learn English in order for them to be able to give them orders more easily. You can imagine the situation where the learner has a need for a particular kind of language that is in conflict with the interests of someone in power. For example, you may find out that one of your students, a woman who is working on the lines, is being sexually harassed by her supervisor. And so what she really needs is the language to complain about the sexual harassment.

One of the informants did not believe that the needs of the learners and the needs of management were always in conflict.

Interview 5: There is usually something in common (between the needs of the workers and the management). You hope to select the needs that maybe have the highest priority. When you ask the learners what they want to do, they always say, "I want to speak better English." The participants usually don't have enough English to express what they need...The supervisor may be able to tell you, "Well, I need people who will punch in. Can you teach this, can you teach that?" And that's wonderful. For example, in the garment industry they said, "We're sewing the wrong labels in the garments for washing instructions. Can you teach the word for colours so that they can get the right label?" Well, that's very explicit, it's very work-related.

This perspective—that there is not necessarily any difference between the needs of management and the needs of the workers—can lead instructors to respond to those needs that are expressed the most clearly and that are seen to have the highest priority—at least from the instructors' perspective, a perspective that is guided by management.

Interview 4: If you look at the way we are trained and the resources we have, we are taught that needs assessment is a tool that amalgamates everybody's needs. We never talk about conflicting needs. Because we depend on management to allow us to hold the classes, to give the workers permission to go to the classes, I think we assume that managers' needs are very important and that they have the workers' best interests at heart. And in meeting management's needs, we also meet workers' needs. And sometimes this may be true. It's important for people to know about health and safety issues, no question. But there are moments when supervisory needs and management needs conflict with workers' needs. Many of us work in factories that are not unionized, you know, and when you talk about what people need language for, in order for people to feel empowered and to participate in a democratic way, what they need is language for unionization. Well, that immediately creates a problem...There is great merit in trying to integrate learners' and management's needs. I don't think they necessarily have to conflict, but we have to be aware that there are tensions there.

This question of assessing needs according to a power differential—in which the needs of management are considered more important than those of the learners—has race implications, even in a unionized setting. The needs of non-whites are likely to be given low priority.

Interview 2: Even if it is a union-initiated program, unions also have their sets of barriers and agendas. And the question is, To what extent is it part of an anti-racist initiative?

The ESL instructor has multiple responsibilities in evaluating and responding to the identified needs.

Interview 7: You want to empower these workers. And you don't really want to make trouble so that they will be denied access to any of these services. And yet you want them to start thinking on the right track. For example, doing the employee handbook with them, they become aware of certain rights. Now is this what the company really wants you to do? Perhaps not. You've got to keep this balance because you don't want to be told not to hold these classes anymore. You have responsibilities towards the workers. You have responsibilities towards your own conscience or philosophy in terms of what you think is right to teach, and you have responsibilities to the person who is paying you and who has the power to cut this off.

The way ESL instructors respond to these multiple responsibilities may depend on their world-views and on the intellectual and personal links they have made between language training and other goals—anti-racism, workers' rights, feminism and human rights issues, among others. Several of the informants identified needs assessment as absolutely key to the effective delivery of language programs. If anti-racism is to be integrated into a workplace program, it is crucial that it be incorporated into the program at the needs assessment stage.

Interview 1: When language is taught in the workplace, I think it should be done only in the context of an organizational needs assessment that identifies the barriers in the organization—including the racial barriers, the ethnocentric barriers, the gender barriers. If you just teach students—assuming you can—how not to be racist in the classroom, then you are blaming the victim and you are setting them up for failure. The entire organization needs to be addressed.

RACIST DISPLAYS

Often, racial conflicts are characterized as cultural differences and misunderstandings. While cultural misunderstandings play a role, inequitable power relations are at the heart of racism. Racial prejudice emerged with the rise of colonialism and capitalism and continues to flourish because of the economic benefits it confers on the dominant white population.

A full understanding of racism must go beyond the model of individual prejudice or discrimination, which is often presented as the essence of racism rather than merely one aspect of it. Nevertheless, these individual manifestations of racism—such as prejudice and discrimination—are extremely significant. Involving more than mere slights, oversights and hurt feelings, they are rightfully seen as part of a complex network of social, economic, political and historical barriers that confine the choices, chances and opportunities of non-whites.

A wide range of behaviour and attitudes in the workplace can be seen as expressions of racism: jokes, slurs, stereotyping, exclusions, and racial and sexual harassment. The Toronto Board of Education defines a racist incident as "an expression, verbal or physical, of racial or ethnic bias; that is, any behaviour, whether or not consciously motivated, which expresses a negative attitude, disparagement, or hatred toward the race, colour, or ethnocultural heritage of a person or group."

The informants were asked to describe incidents of racism that had occurred in their ESL classes.

Interview 1: I can remember a white student refusing to sit with a person of colour. He didn't say it was because it was a person of colour. One just suspected it. You try to partner people up in the classroom for an activity, and he would say, "I'm not sitting with him."...I wouldn't force him. But I would do some kind of empathy-raising exercise.

Interview 5: I had a student who got up and told the class that all the cockroaches in North Toronto were because the Pakistanis had immigrated into Canada. I've had students refusing to work with other students because they were Black, Asian or Pakistani. I think racism appears mostly in students not wanting to work with other students.

Interview 4: There are racial slurs. There are racist jokes and sexist jokes. There are a whole range of things under the rubric of harassment that happen to people at work, just like they happen to people at schools, and in other places as well.

Interview 7: Having lived in a number of different countries, I know that racism here does not always take the overt form that it might take in many countries. It has been my own personal experience that it manifests itself in this country in much more subtle forms, that are often very hard to pinpoint. Say, for example, if you are looking at somebody, the eyes are telling you something. But you can't really confront a person. You can't say, "Well look, this is the feeling I'm getting." You can't put your finger on it. But it is there. As a minority myself, I would rather it came out. But people are hiding their anger and suppressing it.

I would tend to address this as a result of power issues. Sometimes, immigrants are taken advantage of. I can tell you about someone I know. For 10 years, she was in a workplace where she couldn't question her pay because she was absolutely terrified of being laid off. She would experience a reduction in pay and not know why. I think a lot of the smaller workplaces are full of that.

Interview 2: I think it is important to distinguish the racial prejudice that takes place among the students from the racism that appears in the power relations between students and teachers, because we are talking about a different type of relationship. Yes, a lot of times the students come in with their own prejudices or problems, but they don't have the power to play them out against each other.

Several of the informants mentioned incidents of racism that take the form of sexual harassment. In one incident, a supervisor used an extremely offensive sexist colloquialism that the worker misunderstood to be a friendly though confusing comment. When she asked the ESL instructor for clarification, she was horrified to learn its meaning.

Interview 2: I had a hard time explaining it to her. When I finally explained what he had said, she was devastated. She was embarrassed and she was in tears. When he had said it, she didn't understand, she just smiled along. It just shows the abuse that ESL speakers have to go through. In this particular case, she took it up with management. The supervisor was reprimanded. But it was not easy.

Racism also appears in the way students respond to their non-white instructors.

Interview 2: Racism has also been internalized sometimes. I have sent a non-white instructor into a program, but the students felt that the instructor didn't fit in with their perceptions of what a "normal" English instructor should be like. They should be white, they should speak English as a first language. It is a very difficult situation to be in, when an instructor has to deal with being discriminated against on the basis of colour and his or her accent.

Like skin colour, accent is a social code with power implications.

Interview 1: I used to be a pronunciation teacher. And I would often find that there were people in the class whose first language was English, but they wanted to change their accent. Sometimes, their boss had told them they wouldn't get a promotion unless they improved their accent, even though they communicated very well. I could understand everything they said, and their grammar may have been virtually perfect. I would try to tell them that the problem wasn't theirs. But they would say, and quite correctly, I won't get a promotion or people laugh at me. I would never find anyone with a Scottish burr in my class. But Indian English is ridiculed commonly. I know some ESL teachers with accents. And I've had students complain about that too. And I've actually seen administration comply with the students and switch the teacher when they should have said, "Sorry, this is what a Canadian accent is, an accent from diverse parts of the world."

There is a close connection between racism and ethnocentricity. Those with an ethnocentric perspective see the dominant ethnic culture as the norm and judge others on how closely they conform to it. Often based on stereotypes and inaccurate or incomplete information, ethnocentricity appears frequently in apparently harmless conversation. Ethnocentricity is premised on a belief in the centrality and superiority of one's own cultural group. Because of this sense of superiority, ethnocentricity inevitably impedes solidarity.

Interview 6: Sometimes people don't think it's racism, they just think it's the truth. You know, it's like saying rain is wet or something. It's just the way life is.

Interview 3: For both racism and sexism the effect is to divide people, to break down any kind of solidarity, any kind of unity, that we are trying to develop in the group. I think that's really important. The purpose of these classes, in addition to learning language, is to build group support where people can feel free to talk about their problems, and talk about how to deal with them. So what comments like that do is break people apart.

It is often difficult to know the best response to a racial incident that occurs within the class. Among the informants, there was widespread agreement about some general guidelines:

■ Respond immediately. Trust your instincts.

- Use clear, specific, direct language and explain how racism affects you.
- Express clear disapproval of the incident, not the person.
- Encourage discussion.
- Include all affected people in the discussion—the perpetrator, the victim, and all witnesses to the incident.
- Draw on others for support.

DEVELOPING EFFECTIVE RESPONSES

The various ways in which the informants analysed the functions and forms of racism in workplace ESL programs quite clearly shaped their methods of responding. One of the informants argued that structural conditions need to be changed in order for anti-racist education to be effective.

> *Interview 6*: I think it's a bit naive to think you can go in there and do a couple of classes on anti-racism and then come out and everything is hunky-dory. I'm not sure how much effect it has. In terms of racist incidents, I think you start with a bottom line, which is you don't allow it. You say this is a no-go area, in terms of racism, sexism and other forms of discrimination. I always say, in every class I teach, "I don't permit this." It's one of the few places where I assert my role as a teacher and say this is not acceptable.

> *Interview 5*: I think people need to realize the power issues. We have been pussyfooting around this for a long time. You know—it's not nice to be racist—this sort of thing. Well, I'm sorry, it's illegal to be racist. There's a power issue here.

While some of the informants responded to racist incidents by explaining Canadian law and culture, others relied on efforts to seek commonality. One inform-ant pointed out that the law does not prohibit racist attitudes and ideas, but rather the behavioural manifestations of racism—discrimination and actions that promote hatred.

> *Interview 1*: When I hear a racist joke, I try to control my anger because I don't think that admonishing and humiliating the student in front of everyone is going to work. But I would tell them quietly that that sort of talk is not allowed under the Human Rights Code of Ontario. One thing you have to do is let people know how they can behave, how they are allowed to behave. And certainly they can't carry on this behaviour in the workplace. This does have implications for the workplace because it is illegal for starters.

> *Interview 6*: Saying that discrimination is illegal, I think that's okay. But I just prefer to say, "In my classroom, I don't like it because it's bad for learning. I prefer to create another atmosphere," instead of saying, "In Canada, we believe this." I don't like the Big Brother aspect of this. It doesn't ring quite true in some ways. But I mean, sure, you can point out the Human Rights Code and all the rest of it. In the workplace, you can point out that in their collective

agreement, there may be a clause that restricts racist, sexist stuff. Maybe you can deal with it that way.

Interview 3: A conversation we were having in class about immigration got very tense. I really thought a lot about how the heck to bring people back together because it really seemed to set people apart. I didn't know how to do it. If we should do it directly, or what we should do. What I decided to do was to keep talking about immigration. I took in an article that came from a union publication. It gave them some information that I thought would be new to them, how the Chinese had been exploited building the railway. I tried to make a space for people to talk about this. Basically, that's the way we did it, we just sort of went on. I felt that it was better not to say, "You know, you're being racist," and come at it from that point of view.

A related approach that is used by several informants is to provide space within the class for the expression of alternative ideas.

Interview 2: If a student has an immediate situation that he or she wants your assistance with, I would tend to get the whole class involved and see if the other participants have similar concerns or problems. I think it is really important to have the "victims" recognize that it is not an individual problem, that other people in the classroom have probably had the same experiences. And it becomes a group experience. In terms of immediate responses, at times you actually get some very good suggestions from other class members. They might have had similar experiences. You can turn it into an ESL exercise. They can share their stories.

Interview 1: There are often specific, direct, sexist remarks. So I might say, "Well, what do the women in the class think of that remark?" Usually that tended to work because as a group they could look at each other and say something.

Whether the racism is occurring within the classroom or the workplace, it is important to make room for the learners' need to challenge and discuss it. All the informants stressed the importance of responding to racist incidents immediately and publicly, even if it is only to say, "I don't agree," and flag the issue for further discussion. Several described how it is essential to attune yourself, to follow your instincts, and to seek support for an anti-racist perspective from within the class and from outside the class setting.

Interview 5: A lot of people aren't going to say they are sexually or racially harassed, but you have to listen to the silence. Listening to silence. And being aware that racism is there and sexism is there. There's discrimination of all sorts. So you have to sort of anticipate it. And don't be afraid to speak up when you find it. If it's illegal harassment, then you report it to the workplace.

Interview 4: That kind of thing has an audience and any response—whether you respond or not—is a message. Everyone else who has heard that comment and has seen you not respond as a leader of the class, then has an idea of what's permissible and not permissible in the class.

Interview 3: In terms of sexism, one incident comes to mind. I was co-facilitating with someone. It was a group of men who had been laid off. We were at a union hall. One of the guys said something about battering, implying it was okay. Right away, my initial reaction was to say, "I don't feel comfortable with that." He backed off and that was it. But I felt that because they were all men, I needed another strategy. So I talked to my co-facilitator and I told him that I felt that they would listen better, hear it, if it came from him, because I knew they felt that I was only saying it because I'm a woman. So that's what happened. He said, "I don't feel comfortable with that comment either." Whenever things like that come up, I've always tried to think in terms of what is the most effective way of getting them to understand the implications of what they are saying. I felt that it was important to hear a man saying it.

Only one of the informants raised the issue of what happens when the teacher is accused of racism.

teacher accused of "racism"

Interview 4: A lot of people ask, "Well, what happens if you're accused of being racist?" This is a fear a lot of teachers have. You know, the feeling is that in these times, it's so easy for a student to call you racist, right? Well, we talk about intentional racism and unintentional racism, intentional discrimination and unintentional discrimination. Lots of this stuff is unconscious and may not be intended, but it is the impact and the consequence of what you say, rather than the intention, that counts. A lot of teachers say that the accusation of racism is such a strong accusation that you immediately want to deny it. We live in a world where this kind of thing is abhorred. You have to find it in yourself to say, "Why are you saying I'm racist?" You have to consider that it may be true. You may not even have realized that you have behaved that way. But for the person who has made the accusation, there is clear evidence that he or she has been treated differently. If you ask why, then you are in a position to evaluate whether there is any truth to the claim. And if you can then find it in yourself to say, "I didn't realize I did that. I'm sorry," then something important has happened.

It's a great gift if you can do that, but it means letting go of power. And you know, one thing about teaching ESL is that teachers have a lot of power. They always speak English better than their students. So if a student raises a difficult question for a teacher, and the teacher doesn't like the question, I've heard teachers correct the grammar or the pronunciation of the student. And that effectively puts the students in their place. I don't think people do it deliberately or consciously. So it seems to me that there is that responsibility to look at that question carefully and ask why, and try to hear the criticism.

INCORPORATING ANTI-RACIST STRATEGIES

Incidents that happen within the class sometimes point out the need to develop continuing strategies and underlying approaches. A response may result from an individual incident, while a strategy may have several broad purposes. A strategy used by all the informants is the developing of codes of conduct with their classes. While offering the immediate function of teaching vocabulary, this strategy—the formulating of group norms or ground rules—also underscores the democratic approach that is required for learner-centred programs and provides the class with an agreed method of resolving conflicts.

Interview 5: Very soon after the course starts, you say, "Okay, how are we going to operate together as a group? We're here to learn English. What are the norms of behaviour that we are going to allow? What is allowable and what is not allowable?" And so they set up rules like, We listen to each other, We don't interrupt. And then as devil's advocate, more or less, I will say, "Well, if someone calls somebody else…(and I'll use a racist term or an ethnic slur), how are we going to handle that?" And we go through the steps of deciding how we would handle it. So ahead of time, we set up an atmosphere in which we have respect for each other, and I don't leave it at that. Respect is a nice little term, but what does respect for each other mean in behavioural terms? So respect means that we listen to each other, that we do not prejudge each other, that we give time before we give a negative or a positive evaluation, that we do not play favourites. I usually type up the group norms. We go back over it the next week, see what we like, what we don't like.

Interview 3: We set up the ground rules governing how we are going to work together beforehand. They might be things like: We respect each other; Each person has a chance to speak and be listened to; We are all equal here; Decisions are made democratically; those kinds of things.

Setting ground rules is only one strategy for creating an atmosphere in which learners are encouraged to respect each other.

Interview 4: Most ESL books start with Chapter 1, Introductions. It's a way of introducing some elementary language and introducing ourselves. Well, there is a book called *ESL for Action, Problem Posing at the Workplace* that shows you how you can do a twist on something very simple. You make a circle with your chairs and say, "My name is so and so. What's your name?" Then you ask if everyone's name is written on the board, and were all the names written correctly and were all names pronounced correctly, which is in itself an anti-racist strategy. Then they have a little dialogue here in the book and it's a dialogue between a supervisor and a Vietnamese worker. (The dialogue referred to demonstrates the power dynamics between the supervisor and the worker: the worker is corrected when he mispronounces the supervisor's name, while the supervisor proceeds to anglicize the worker's name.) So the issue is problematized, right? The language is not all that difficult, but the issue is very meaningful. It would be a situation that people who have experienced it would get right away.

Interview 1: A standard exercise is to ask people to set up an informal conversation where they explain how they got to Canada, what were their stories. And so I remember people from Central Europe talking about arriving very comfortably in Canada, and others talking about their boat stories, for example. And you could see that the Europeans who had to hear these terrible stories would learn to empathize with these people who were, of course, people of colour, like people from Vietnam. So sharing stories is one way to make it work.

Exercises such as this are useful devices for encouraging conversation and empathetic exchanges and establishing an atmosphere of respect, but some of the informants questioned whether they are effective anti-racist strategies by themselves. They believe that a holistic, comprehensive approach is necessary.

Some key points that emerged from the discussions about strategies were:

- The absolutely crucial importance of integrating an anti-racist approach throughout the curriculum.
- The significance of analysing issues with racial content and power implications (as the arrival and introduction exercises are in the preceding examples).
- The value of teaching the language of resistance (including a variety of options for responding to illegal harassment and discrimination) as the means, the method, and the focus for empowering ESL learners.

Interview 2: The issue is more complex than just trying to provide a few tools, a blueprint, and have it attached as the end chapter of a book. Racism is part of the workplace culture. It's part of the whole organizational, institutionalized discrimination.

Interview 6: One of the problems that I have about this way of doing anti-racist education with ESL students is that often we are doing anti-racist education among the ESL students who are the people who face racism in their everyday lives, who in some ways don't need a lot of anti-racism education about it because they experience it in lots of ways.

What I see is a need to permeate the curriculum materials with stuff so it's in there. So it's not a block of time, where for one week out of 14, we devote time to racism. Instead, it's implicit in the whole class. I would say that you need to go through the program, the materials, and the curriculum, to see that everything within it is anti-racist, anti-sexist, and anti-class.

Interview 7: It goes a lot deeper than just language. The language is very important. It's a very strong tool in your hand. But it doesn't begin and end there. First of all, they've got to become aware of their rights. Not only become aware of them, but actually fight for them.

Interview 3: I think it's important to talk about things that are relevant to their lives. I mean talking about things like 500 Years of Resistance, talking about Native issues, making connections. Keeping an eye on what the issues are that are current. I remember when the firefighters were instituting an equity program. I brought that information to the ESL class. I was working with a group of Caribbean men. So it was really relevant to them.

Interview 6: I know a lot of classes where they deal with ESL skills, where people learn office skills and typing and this kind of stuff. And the language that they don't teach, and I really think they should, is language that deals with sexual harassment. Most of these people are women and most are looking for skills for entry-level office jobs. In order to survive in the working world, it is not a bad idea to have some idea of sexual harassment—the laws, the culture, what it means if someone touches you, what you can do about it.

A lot of the anti-racist, anti-sexist stuff, I don't really like very much, a lot of it doesn't do very much in terms of real action responses. A lot of it is kind of "write to the Human Rights Commission" type of response. And you think, Well okay, that'll be four years before it comes to anything. But at least it's a step that you do something—you write a letter. I think one can work out, with the students, a series of alternative responses. So this person said this to this woman, so what can she do next time? She can say, "Back off, jerk," or she can say, "I don't like that." Or she can keep quiet. With one, she may lose her job, one she may keep her job. So which one? She can decide what she wants to do. But the focus has to be on language. Not just because that's what we do, but because it's what people need, too. They need the language of responses.

CHALLENGING STRUCTURAL CONDITIONS

A central issue in the anti-racism pursuit is the need to identify and challenge the structural conditions that perpetuate racism. Several of the instructors mentioned the need for major improvement in two areas: more support and training for all ESL instructors, and an increase in the numbers of non-white ESL teachers.

Interview 2: There are some white instructors who come in with almost a missionary attitude. They are coming in to "help." They feel these are the helpless immigrant women workers. They have a very paternalistic attitude.

Maybe they need anti-racism training. They need to know their own positions in the society and recognize that being white gives them a certain advantage, and that in the power hierarchy within the society they are in a more advantageous position than the participants. But it's important that they move beyond guilt. If you can turn that situation around, turn your advantageous position to work for the benefit of the anti-racism movement, then it is using power in a positive fashion.

We need teachers from different cultural backgrounds, diverse backgrounds, and teachers of colour. As minority people, we are confronted with racism on a daily basis. So where do we get white instructors to develop that sense of empathy? And second, it's empathy without a patronizing attitude. And then, third, it's recognizing where the workers are, where the participants are. Yes, we want more instructors of colour, but at the same time, we don't want to be relegated to being "experts" on these issues. Because then racism is only our responsibility, when it should be a shared responsibility.

I think it's important to have instructors of colour, non-white instructors. Their presence provides some sort of role model. However, we can't make the assumption that non-white instructors would automatically be activists in the anti-racism movement. They might have a different sense of where they are at. Some would say, "I don't need employment equity, I don't need any of this, I can make it on my own."

Interview 5: I think there needs to be more training for teachers in dealing with this. I think there needs to be more openness, more communication.

Interview 3: The other thing that we have to keep doing—that I have to keep doing—is we have to continually educate ourselves around this issue, and around how to respond to it. I think there really is a resistance by white ESL teachers to this issue, even to acknowledge our own baggage. So I think we have to deal with that first.

Interview 6: One of the problems in most ESL programs is that it tends to be a part-time, temporary kind of thing. If someone is working four or six hours a week, then it's hard to bring them in for more training. It's not the main part of their work in life. They're not getting paid much for it. So I would argue that there should be a move to professionalize it and to make it more full-time.

What else? I think there should be a revamping of the whole needs assessment aspect, because I think a lot of times we don't touch on what people need. And this includes racism, sexism, all that, but it includes a lot of other things. Power issues and also other issues. I don't think there is a book about how to talk to your kids' teachers. We don't consider people's real lives.

I think there is a lack of materials dealing with racism and sexism. Where can you find something dealing with how to respond to sexual harassment?

Teachers need to know a lot more about issues of race and gender, issues of class. They need to have these issues built into their teaching training a lot more. They need more workshops, more in-service training. And, again, if you professionalize the industry, then you can do a lot better.

Interview 4: ESL teachers need a sense of community. They need professional development opportunities. A lot of ESL teachers will tell you that they feel very alone. And they need more anti-racist materials. Often what happens is that consultants are hired to develop material and they learn a lot from the process. They get financial rewards and they learn from it. But if the teachers themselves aren't involved in developing the curriculum, then it's not a part of them. It's something else on the shelf. People need training and they need development opportunities. For me, the key to unravelling a lot of this stuff has do with the questioning of assumptions and the unlearning of the taken-for-granted assumptions. We need to challenge ourselves to look critically at our assumptions. The more we can question our assumptions, the more we can listen to other people's experiences, the more we can link lived experiences to structural, social, economic and political relations in society, the better off we are.

CONCLUSION

Several of the informants identified attitude as the single most important ingredient in creating an anti-racist ESL class. But they all emphasized that good intentions alone are not enough. Good intentions must be combined with detailed knowledge of and information about racism, an empathetic understanding of the impact of racism, experience with effective strategies, a comprehensive anti-racism curriculum and teaching materials, and the humility and commitment to first learn, and then teach, the language of resistance.

CHAPTER 11

The Study at Work Trailer: An Interview

by Mary Ellen Belfiore
with Christina Pikios

In this interview, Christina Pikios, an educational consultant with Workplace Training Systems at the Open Learning Agency in Burnaby, British Columbia, describes the process, successes and frustrations of setting up a workplace education project in a sawmill. The Study at Work (SAW) Trailer was set up at the mill to house various educational programs ranging from ESL literacy to computer-simulated millwork.

THE INTERVIEW

Belfiore: How does the workplace context determine the kind of education your agency offers?

Pikios: The needs and dynamic of a workplace set the stage. Before we set up a program, we have to know why we are there, and why and if there is a need in that workplace. It's a much broader picture than speaking English better or doing math better.

We are promoting a type of understanding and a type of learning that was never equated with the workplace. In the past, once you got a job you were really secure—you met your goal. But that's no longer the case. Most of the people had the skills they needed when they first went into this work, but the goals keep changing now—the goalposts keep getting moved. Whose ethical responsibility is it to maintain and upgrade skills? It's a shared responsibility between the employers, union, employees, government and educational institutions. With this set of realities, think how much pressure there is on all these players around issues like retraining and seniority.

Seniority is the biggest issue at this sawmill with regard to retraining and further education. For example, an older worker has seniority and is eligible for training but, because of his age, he doesn't want to take the training. There's a younger worker who has the current skills, but he's low on the seniority list. If he's asked to help train the older worker, he's resistant. He knows that if a better job comes up, he won't get it because the worker with more seniority—whom he helped train—will be eligible, not him. The employer feels that he needs to hire trained people but also knows that he has to promote internally—how does he do it? The company and union are in constant grievances over this issue.

Belfiore: You mentioned that the model of the general adult education class doesn't fit into workplaces. What does your workforce skills upgrading program try to do that's different?

Pikios: We believe it's important to develop a very flexible, integrated training model that meets a cross-section of needs. The reality is that, as adults, we don't have homogeneous skill levels or needs. There could be one individual who comes in with high reading and math skills but low writing skills. If we ask him to spend hours on what he already knows, it won't work. For the same reasons, a worker going back to a traditional school setting often has to do a full spectrum of study when he needs concentrated work only in specific areas. Or he finds he has to take a year of study in math, when all he really needs is a month or two to upgrade his skills.

A large number of workers at the mill need computer awareness and computer skills. It's wonderful when you can integrate the work-related training with computer skills. The company came up with an idea for an employee-purchase plan for computers. So far, about 30 employees have purchased their own home computers. They are working on educational programs at home and helping their kids more, too. One supervisor reports that one of his men who used to be frightened of even touching the keyboard can now work with a keyboard and does his job a lot better.

So, we have to move from a teacher-centred or course-centred curriculum to an individualized curriculum. You still have basic generic areas to cover but we have different learning styles, different time demands. The two instructors here work split shifts from 7:30 in the morning through the evening. No one shows up on Friday so there aren't any instructors that day. It's the company work reality that drives how you are going to set up the program. A mistake people often make is that they try to take a successful model in one workplace and transfer that format to another workplace. That second workplace doesn't have the same history, the same people, the same shifts—it isn't going to work out.

On an individual basis, you have to ask what people's strengths, needs and goals are. The goals are a combination of work-related and personal goals.

In the trailer, there is also the challenge of hiring facilitators and instructors who can work together and enhance and complement each other. We talk about the multi-skilling or cross-skilling of the workforce, but there is also the cross-skilling and multi-skilling of our instructors.

Belfiore: Could you explain what you mean by cross-skilling and why you think it's important in training instructors?

Pikios: Cross-skilling of teachers is essential. At the mill, one instructor is experienced in adult basic education and the other has an ESL certificate and used to work at the mill 20 years ago. He has lived in the community and done industry training as well as computer training.

I think we'll see more linkages with trades trainers in the future. ESL is now just one small component of workplace training programs.

I would like to look at the German model where language instructors also train in a trade. When they graduate, they have both a trade ticket and language training to offer. Instructors need to be flexible, unafraid of technology and willing to work in a cross-skilled environment.

Maturity is also an important element. Instructors need maturity and a secure sense of themselves and of their field to manage in these difficult and diverse workplaces. Along the same lines, they need more communication skills because there isn't the support group that normally exists in an educational institution. How do they understand and fit into the infrastructure and mindsets of different workplaces?

Switching from a classroom to a workplace, instructors are no longer the main focus but part of a team. This teamwork requires knowledge of union and management practices, not to mention conflict resolution skills such as negotiating, mediating and just being a good listener. When learners start swearing at you, you have to feel secure enough to realize that they aren't attacking you as a person, but swearing out of frustration.

Belfiore: How did the Workforce Training Program get involved in this sawmill?

Pikios: The sawmill had an industrial adjustment service committee (IAS—a federal government service that provides financial incentives to help employers and workers make adjustments to employment necessitated by economic, technological or structural change) that was set up to help the mill with the changes in the industry. There were changes in technology—an increase in the level of technology and computers throughout the mill; in the market—cutting to Japanese standards from American and European; and in the downsizing of the workforce because of these innovations. The older workers maintained their jobs because of seniority, but their skills could not meet the demands of the changing market.

Belfiore: What's unique about the educational project at this sawmill?

Pikios: First of all, it's in the lumber industry. Setting up a program at a sawmill—there's not much to compare it to. Second, the large size of the needs assessment in this company allowed us to talk to quite a number of people. Third, management-union relationships and relations within the union are unusual. Usually, the union buys in or not. Here, a high-level union stakeholder is not supportive, but the union members are supportive and the local office is supportive. So, we're fighting these dynamics. The workforce is 48 per cent Punjabi-speaking, which creates a real division. It is also a stable and aging workforce that has a long history and a lot of baggage.

In terms of the content of our educational program, we expanded our philosophy, which combines an integrated approach with individualized learning. Here, we've integrated a variety of areas that haven't been offered simultaneously before: basic literacy, ESL, adult basic education, secondary school diploma, specific work-skills training, computer introduction, computer processing, and the flexibility to introduce other kinds of training as the needs arise. For instance, in the trailer, we are just introducing a computer edger simulation program that is job-specific and enables a completely different group of employees to participate in the program.

The program is very individualized. Assessment can be 10 to 20 hours for each person. The instructor sits down with the person to discuss immediate goals. Some people might be working on math, reading and computer skills at the same time. If we have four people working on one area at the same time, we hold mini-workshops as we did with the introduction to computers. Some workers need just math, others want their secondary school graduation certificate to become millwrights and some want special programs for changes in the industry. It's very integrated.

Belfiore: What training is specifically work-related?

Pikios: Some of the math is work-related as well as the computer programs, especially the simulated edger program. As for language skills, we've analysed what writing skills are necessary in that workplace and we're working on those.

Belfiore: What parts of the workforce are participating in the program and what areas have people shown most interest in?

Pikios: We have people from all sections of the mill, even the office staff who are taking computer applications. About 100 people have used the trailer facilities on either a regular or temporary basis.

Employees have shown the most interest in computers, especially word processing. There's also been a lot of interest in math, reading and writing, analytical or critical thinking and learning how to learn.

For me, this is an excellent example of how workplace training affects the culture of a workplace—introducing a continuing training culture and all the dynamics that are part of the process. We are not segregating one group of workers out for training. We are saying, instead, that training cuts across the whole spectrum of the workplace. That's unique. The trailer is on the worksite. All the men who are signed up in the program have a key to the trailer so they have access to the trailer when they can be there, and not just when the instructors can be there. It allows for flexibility and accessibility on all three shifts.

Belfiore: How do the workers see this trailer?

Pikios: Some are very enthusiastic and supportive and see it as an opportunity for themselves, not just for this workplace but for going beyond it. We have a number of men who are doing math upgrading so they can do accounting in small business management. They want to get out of the industry because they see with downsizing that there isn't security any longer. Some men see it as a chance to change their jobs within the company because age or health problems will not allow them to keep their same position. Others feel threatened by it; it's not part of their reality.

One man who was on long-term disability now has his self-esteem back and new jobs have been created for him. He's now a tour guide for the mill, a job the human resources manager doesn't have time for anymore. He loves it, especially working with the schoolchildren. He's become more of a PR person now and the company is also saving a lot of money having him off disability payments.

In terms of personal success stories, men are finding they are able to deal with their children better, they work with them more, and are generally feeling better about what they are capable of at work and at home.

Belfiore: What specifically do the supervisors mean when they say people are working better?

Pikios: People feel more comfortable doing their jobs; they are understanding and following instructions better; they work faster and fewer mistakes are made. Supervisors are getting more reports when machinery breaks down or is not working well because the men realize now it's not their fault and have the confidence to report it. Overall, I see that people are much more involved in the company and taking an active part in it. It's very positive.

Belfiore: So, the program has been a unifying force at the mill?

Pikios: Yes, although I don't think we were the only influence. There are a number of in-house committees that have been gaining momentum.

This Christmas, the mill had its first holiday party in 18 years. Two of the men who were instrumental in getting this program off the ground were recognized at the party for the work they had done in this program. It seems that the trailer was a major influence in having the party and bringing people together. There are many small successes like these that are hard to measure.

Belfiore: What about your role as educators and walking the line between management and the union?

Pikios: As educators, we have to take a neutral role, which means not being readily identified as pro-union or as pro-management.

Belfiore: Would you say you are pro-worker?

Pikios: Pro-worker? What does that mean? We have to establish who we are and what we are there for. We are experts in workplace upgrading and our role is to identify what that is and there are different issues to contend with in each workplace. Our role is to listen to every side and, using our expertise as educators, analyse the situation and come up with a delivery plan that will fit the best. Quite often, we have to be negotiators and mediators and that means letting them take the lead.

Belfiore: How did you "let them take the lead" at this mill?

Pikios: In terms of expanding the program to other components of the company, the company took the lead. But in letting people set their own direction, there have to be guidelines and we have to ensure that all the sides are listening. We can learn from each other what these directions should be and how to set them in motion. We are each coming from our own limited perspective. To find out how the perspectives fit and how they can be expanded, we have to communicate with each other in the fullest sense of the word.

In a big industry like lumber, we can't be limited to thinking in terms of one workplace. We have to consider what the issues are in the whole industry. To become knowledgeable about these issues, we need help from the people in the industry so that our training perspective is always in the context of the whole industry. Sometimes, as educators, we make a mistake by coming in with our own perspective and that's it.

Belfiore: You mentioned that you have to work through a process with a company. Let's talk more about the overall process of setting up an educational program in a workplace.

Pikios: At this sawmill, I think our process was a very good one. The questionnaire for the needs assessment was developed with the advisory committee, not by us alone, and it was changed, developed and field-tested before it was finally adopted by the committee. Because all the key stakeholders worked together at this first level, every group bought in. We worked with the committee to decide how many people we would involve in the needs assessment and how we would interview them—in focus groups, individually or an anonymous questionnaire. The focus groups were particularly successful because they provided avenues for people to express their concerns in a less threatening group atmosphere with people they knew. Also, individuals with very strong and opinionated views often found they had to moderate them because the group was not prepared to accept these ideas unconditionally. The needs assessment works on several levels. We're doing public relations work, giving people a chance to find out what the process involves and opening up new ideas and thoughts. It would be good to do some initial focus groups and then come back two or three weeks later so that people have a chance to think about their responses and move even farther along. In this way, the needs assessment would be two or three steps rather than just one and help everyone get used to the idea of continuing education.

Belfiore: In this workplace, you did a job task analysis as part of the needs assessment. Why did you decide to include it at this stage?

Pikios: I think the job task analysis is essential. What jobs are done there? What changes have taken place and do the men see that there has been a change in what is demanded of them? Often, people will say that they don't see any difference in their jobs now. Perhaps we need to help them see the differences and the new demands or perhaps we need to deal with their resistance and fear. So, in a job task analysis, we are raising awareness, answering a lot of questions and learning a great deal about the industry.

Belfiore: What issues came up in the needs assessment—especially the issues you didn't expect to find?

Pikios: The main issues are the relationship between union and management, the history of the workplace, the factions that have divided this workplace, and racism. Half the workforce is non-white, but the organization maintained that racism was not an issue. We were thanked by one of the Punjabi members of the committee for putting down on paper for the first time that racism *is* a problem at this workplace. A number of people were hoping we wouldn't mention this issue and others were nervous about how we would handle it.

Belfiore: How have you dealt with the issue of racism and changing perceptions?

Pikios: To begin with, I was asked to give a workshop on cross-cultural or diversity training but they wanted to just call it communications.

We need to bring more representatives on to our committee from the different religious groups at the mill. We've learned here and in other workplaces that it's important to identify and then get to know the groups or factions that make up the workforce. Then, for the program to be supported and maintained, we need representation from as many groups as possible on our advisory committee. If calling the workshop "communications training" will draw in more people, that's fine.

Let me give you an example of why knowing the history of a place is important in dealing with the issues; in this case, with the issue of racism. About 12 years ago, the mill was going through a difficult time and a large number of men were laid off. The employees were given a choice. They could either remain with the mill but put up with half-time work and layoffs while maintaining their seniority or resign their positions and look for work elsewhere. Most of the people who decided to leave were white, while the East Indian population decided to remain with the mill. Four of five years later, when the mill started picking up again, the white workers came back and found that the East Indians who had put up with the insecurity over those years now had more seniority than they did, a reversal of the situation the white workers had known. That's the backdrop to cross-cultural training here.

Belfiore: The initial needs assessment process certainly gives you an opportunity to meet a cross-section of the workplace. How do you keep finding out more about the workers and their alliances once the program is under way?

Pikios: We have to be receptive and flexible in the design of the program because, as more people get involved in training, different issues begin to emerge. How receptive are we to change the program so that it fits the reality of a changing workplace? Formative and summative evaluations are critical in keeping the program flexible and receptive. I always used to say that, but I don't think I ever believed it as much as I believe it now.

Belfiore: What happened to make you reach this understanding?

Pikios: The program started to take on a life of its own as people began to come regularly and identify with it. Then, people's expectations grew to the point that they felt the trailer could answer all their problems. Expectations about what we could deliver were getting completely out of hand.

We became the neutral zone for complaints about supervisors, management or the union and workers expected us to counsel, advise and fix things up. We do offer some counselling but we can't replace the human resources office. The manager of human resources had also become so overloaded that he would give us more and more activities to take over. Everyone wanted the trailer to become what they wanted it to be. Some of our education committee members got burned out as the workload increased and then we had to step back to reassess our role in this workplace.

It was essential for us to go back to our training proposal and review our objectives. I sat down with the instructors, the education committee and some learners and we evaluated how well we were meeting those objectives. We listed the actions that had been taken on each objective, the time required and, finally, forecasts for the next three or four months. We then reported back to the general advisory committee with a better definition of what our responsibilities at the workplace were.

Belfiore: Could you talk about one of the objectives that needed more of your attention?

Pikios: Let's take the ESL group. We were hoping to get more of the ESL workers to come into the trailer. They weren't coming and we had to ask why. It turned out we hadn't asked the right stakeholders to support us. We had to find out about the different factions in the workplace and the different groups within the East Indian community based on religious or historical ties. We had to identify who the key players were in this community to bring these workers in. We hadn't nurtured our relationship with these groups or their leaders and that's what it takes in a large workplace like this one. It's all about the power structure.

Now, we are dealing with all the different stakeholders, slowly building our relationships. We do a good job with each person who comes into the trailer and follow up by asking her or him to help spread the word about using the trailer and our services. We also have information packages translated into Punjabi. The human resources manager asked me recently to get some medical insurance information translated and that was the first time the mill translated anything of that level into Punjabi.

Belfiore: Your message seems to be to let things develop slowly. Your training proposal was for 19 months. What factors made your project a program lasting nearly two years?

Pikios: The first proposal was to take in 20 people every three months and to consider about 100 people. Realistically, I didn't think we could go so fast or take in so many people at once. You have to get buy-in by starting with a few people and then develop more and more of a clientele. I wanted two years; they wanted one year so we settled for 19 months.

If everyone is given an individual assessment when they start the program, we could have up to 20 hours of assessment. In a workplace, we have to establish trust for people to open up about their educational needs and only then can we figure out what levels people are at. If we are using a computer to do the assessment, then we need time to teach people how to use the computer so that the results are accurate. Also, at this mill, the program is 100 per cent volunteer time, which means we need more time for recruiting and completing programs. Taking all these factors into consideration, I don't see how we could have a successful program in a shorter time.

Belfiore: Because this is all on volunteer time, how is the company demonstrating support for the program?

Pikios: The company is paying 50 per cent of the costs and the federal government is paying 50 per cent. The costs include renting and setting up the trailer, the materials, the instructors' salaries, office bills, etc. The total cost for the program is $170,000. It certainly is a commitment on the company's part and they may put in more as we develop.

Belfiore: You've been running for seven months now. What about the next 12 months and beyond?

Pikios: We need to keep asking what people need and if they are progressing. We have a logical laddering process for organizing educational programs so that most people will eventually get access to the programs they want. For instance, if people want to take a computer program, they have to have a certain reading level before they can have access to those courses.

We also use the computer as a hook to draw people in. Very few adults say they want to upgrade their reading skills; rather, they say they want to learn to use a computer. In the process of learning to use the computer, we help them improve their reading skills.

In the long term, we would like to see the trailer become a permanent training site at the mill. It could be used for all types of training, including health and safety.

Belfiore: Let's talk about the role of the instructor.

Pikios: We see the role as a facilitator-instructor. I see the instructor as someone who knows information and content and, because of the integration of skills and the design of the program, quite often this person is also a facilitator; that is, he or she shows people how to do things for themselves, how to get information, and is also flexible enough to work in different areas. They are also called upon to work with the education committee, talk to workers and management and generally facilitate the whole process of education at the worksite.

I make it very clear to the company and the instructors who deals with particular problems. It's important to enable the instructors to gain the credibility and respect they need for the program to be successful.

Belfiore: What is it like to be a woman in a predominantly male workforce?

Pikios: The female teacher was concerned initially about feeling isolated, the reaction she would get from the men and the lack of female support. She has gotten used to the workplace now and it's not as much of an issue any longer.

As for myself, I felt fine realizing that the problem was not mine but theirs. The challenge for me as a female is how much I adapt to what they want me to be. The more I see they want me to do that, the less I want to adapt. They have to take me for who I am.

Belfiore: What partnerships have been formed during the process of setting up and implementing the training program?

Pikios: "Partnerships" is a key word in programs like these where educational institutions are not just waiting for people to come to them. Formal partnerships have been formed between the educational institution and many different levels within the company. Within the company, lateral partnerships have developed with individuals in different departments, both formal and informal. Of course, partnerships with external funders like the federal government have also been formed. When we talk about partnerships, we often mean relationship-building, which is essential when we talk to all the various sides to find out what the needs are. Education is coming to terms with being a business where partnerships have always been a reality. Neither educators nor businesspeople have all the answers, so we are faced with the challenge of moving forward by working together.

Belfiore: Can you give some examples of how new partnerships have changed life at the mill or changed people's life circumstances?

Pikios: These new partnerships have brought people together to communicate, sometimes for the first time. As a consequence, there was the first-ever Christmas party at the mill. Committees have drawn people into their work who never were involved before. The office staff, mostly women, had never participated with the men before on common work and now are part of the committees. People who have never worked together before are now co-operating with each other through this partnership.

The employee computer-purchase program is another example. Staff came from head office to do the PR work and locate all the local resources that could supply the computers. This purchase program also built up a partnership with the small community that is home for the mill by using local retailers and bringing money back into the community.

The whole process has brought together people who traditionally would not have had much contact, even though they may have been part of the same company or community.

CHAPTER 12 # Clear Language Documents for the Workplace

by Corinna Frattini

A 1990 Statistics Canada survey revealed that 38 per cent of Canadians between the ages of 16 and 69 have some degree of difficulty reading, writing and communicating. Twenty-two per cent of those Canadians are able to read only very simple, clearly designed documents. Given these statistics, the use of clear language is vital in any workplace environment.

The use of clear language in the workplace is one of many options available to organizations interested in improving the reading skills of employees. Clear language can help improve people's access to information regardless of their reading level or education.

Understanding the basic principles of clear language and document design helps writers meet the needs of their intended audience.

This chapter examines:

- Clear language and its importance for the workplace.
- Clear writing guidelines.
- Readability testing.
- Principles of document design as it relates to workplace materials.

WHAT IS CLEAR LANGUAGE?

Clear language is the use of plain and concise words that help people from a variety of areas and backgrounds understand your message. It is essential to know your audience if you want to communicate effectively. The choice of words must reflect the reader's culture, education level, employment, income level, sex, race and family structure.

WHY IS CLEAR LANGUAGE IMPORTANT?

Canadian employees are now required to read more information to meet the daily demands of their jobs. In addition, many documents are written at a level that exceeds employees' reading and comprehension ability.

JOB-RELATED LITERACY SKILLS

Clear language is essential at the workplace where employees are required to know, understand and act upon important information. This material may include:

- Employee training information.
- Health and safety information.
- Company policies and procedures.
- Collective agreements.
- Operating instructions.
- Memos and other correspondence.

Today, few jobs require limited reading. With the rapid rate of technological change, employees must constantly stay abreast of new information. Employee training is taking on greater significance as organizations try to adapt to a changing business world. Proficient reading, writing and communication skills are essential if employees are to manage this change and meet rising skill requirements.

Organizations can assist their employees by paying attention to their written communication strategies. Documents that are filled with technical jargon, legalese and gobbledegook serve only to complicate a message. Important information must be presented in a manner that people understand if they are to stay healthy, safe and effective.

The design of a document also improves its readability. If it is appealing to the eye, the reader will make a greater effort to read it. Design principles such as ample white space, descriptive headings and appropriate typeface and font selections help create visual appeal.

HOW CAN CLEAR LANGUAGE HELP?

Clear language can help all employees within an organization, not just those with low reading skills. It will also help employees who are learning English as a second language. Difficult language is a communication barrier for all. Clear language and visual appeal encourage people to read important documents.

WHAT WILL CLEAR WRITING DO?

1. Clear writing reduces the word count in a sentence. Long sentences and complex phrases can confuse the reader and cloud the message. Long, wordy phrases can often be replaced by a single word—or omitted entirely. Here are some examples:

   - With regard to—about
   - Afford an opportunity—enable
   - With the exception of—except for
   - In consequence of—because
   - In an effort to—to

2. Clear writing reduces word length (in syllables). When prefixes (such as pro-, anti-, ad-, ab-, ex- and con-) or suffixes (such as -ing, -ed, -ate, -ion, -ite and -ize) are added to a root word, it can become more complex to the reader. The word "operat(e)-ion-al-ize" is a good example.

3. Clear writing restores action to sentences. Active verbs have much more impact than passive ones. The sentence should do what you want your readers to do.

4. Clear writing speaks directly to the reader. This avoids confusion.

BASIC PRINCIPLES OF CLEAR WRITING

Effective writing is simple and straightforward. There is no need to confuse a reader with long sentences, empty phrases or unfamiliar terminology.

THE CLEAR WRITER'S CHECKLIST

These are guidelines for clear writing.

1. Write directly to your reader. Avoid the third person.
   This applies to both the text and the salutation (e.g. "Dear…" or "To:"). If your readers are not sure that you are writing to them directly, they may not understand the message. Avoid the third person.

   - First person: I, we, us, mine, etc.
   - Second person: you, your, yours, etc.
   - Third person: they, all employees, all staff, them, etc.

   For example:

   Before Clear Language

   All employees are required to list flawed products in the work log at the end of each hour of work.

After Clear Language

To: All Employees
Please list all flawed products in your work log after every hour you work.

2. Don't change verbs into nouns.

Doing so clutters sentences and makes them less dynamic.

Verbs	*Nouns*
decide	decision
determine	determination
examine	examination
inspect	inspection
direct	direction

For example:

Before Clear Language

All decisions about the dispensation of subsidies for outside education will be the prerogative of the president's office.

After Clear Language

The president will decide whether the company will pay for your outside courses.

3. Write instructions in the order you want them carried out.

If you have small children who are learning how to talk, you already know this. If you say to your toddler, "Before you go to bed, remember to brush your teeth," you may find her in bed with her toothbrush. Instead you might say, "Brush your teeth before you go to bed."

For example:

Before Clear Language

Before returning your time sheets, please make sure they have been authorized by your supervisor.

After Clear Language

Ask your supervisor to authorize your time sheets before you turn them in.

4. Use the active voice.

In sentences written in the passive voice, the "doer" of the action is unknown. This may be confusing for people who have trouble reading. It is also confusing for people who are learning English, because some other languages do not have a similar structure. Passive constructions are often weak and awkward and should be replaced by the more direct active voice. There are times, however, when using the passive voice makes sense, especially when the "doer" *is* unknown or unimportant.

Passive Voice	*Active Voice*
The lead wires must be checked...	Check the lead wires...
The office phone is not to be used...	Do not use...

For example:

Before Clear Language

The coffee pot must be washed every Monday, Wednesday and Friday.

After Clear Language

Please make sure that you wash the coffee pot every Monday, Wednesday and Friday.

5. Write complete sentences only when it makes sense to do so.

Years of schooling taught us that we must write everything in complete sentences. So, if the examination question read, "When was the War of 1812 fought?" we dutifully wrote, "The War of 1812 was fought..."

For example:

Before Clear Language

The normal working day begins at 9 a.m. and ends at 5 p.m. There are two coffee breaks, lasting 15 minutes apiece, at 10:15 a.m. and 3:15 p.m. Lunch periods are 60 minutes and begin at 12 noon.

After Clear Language

9 a.m.	Work begins
10:15 to 10:30 a.m.	Coffee break
12 to 1 p.m.	Lunch
3:15 to 3:30 p.m.	Coffee break
5 p.m.	Work day ends

6. Highlight critical information outside the text.

Burying important details, such as dates, times and places, inside a paragraph is a leading cause of missed meetings.

For example:

Before Clear Language

All employees are requested to return the enclosed reply cards by the due date, stating their interest in attending a company golf tournament on June 17.

The tournament will be held at the Horseshoe Valley Golf Club and should be an ideal morale booster for the entire organization.

The company will cover half the costs of golfing and the dinner following the tournament, so that each employee will be requested to pay $20 for the day...

After Clear Language

First Annual Company Golf Tournament

Date:	June 17, 1995
Place:	Horseshoe Valley Golf Club
Price:	$20 (The company will pay the other $20)
Sign-up:	By May 31, 1995
For more information:	Call Susan at personnel (Extension 324).

7. List items in a parallel (the same grammatical) form.

Strictly speaking, this is a more correct style of writing. More important, using parallel structures helps your readers find the meaning of the written material more quickly because they do not need to decode as much information.

For example:

Before Clear Language

Employees made the following suggestions to the employee suggestion box:
Redesign of the paint line.
Moving the water cooler to the employee lounge.
Let's have the Christmas party at the Holiday Inn.

After Clear Language

Employees suggested the following changes this month:
Redesign the paint line.
Move the water cooler to the employee lounge.
Hold the Christmas party at the Holiday Inn.

You could also write...

To redesign the paint line.
To move the water cooler to the employee lounge.
To hold the Christmas party at the Holiday Inn.

8. Use a positive tone whenever possible.

A negative tone turns readers off. Perhaps you are writing in a negative fashion because something went wrong. It is better to tell people what you want them to do, rather than what you do not want them to do. Adopt a courteous tone to avoid offending readers.

For example:

Before Clear Language

Do not place mileage expense forms in the travel expense file.

After Clear Language

Place mileage expense forms in the mileage forms file, not in the travel expense file.

9. Avoid using jargon.

Every profession, job, trade or field of interest has its own unique vocabulary. Many have their own way of writing. This sometimes works well when they are communicating with others in the same profession. The problem occurs when they use jargon to communicate with someone outside the field. Often, jargon is unnecessary, but writers use it thinking it will make them sound official, important or in-the-know.

For example:

Before Clear Language

Strict and vigilant compliance with the aforementioned safety regulations will ensure the continued health and safety of all concerned.

After Clear Language

Please follow these rules carefully for your safety and your coworkers' safety.

10. Explain difficult words in their context.

Difficult words are not simply long or technical vocabulary. They can be words that have a very specific meaning in a given context. Explaining involves more than simply giving a definition. It involves finding a way of relating the word to your reader's experience.

For example:

Before Clear Language

Make sure the grapplesnappits are securely flanged.

After Clear Language

Make sure the lids (grapplesnappits) are securely sealed, using the flanging machine.

READABILITY TESTING

Readability tests help assess the grade level of a document based on the number of words in sentences and the number of syllables in words. Various readability tests are available; however, users should be aware of the limitations of grade-level testing. A readability formula may tell you whether you have a problem, but it doesn't tell you how to solve it. Nevertheless, readability tests are useful if you wish to survey the reading materials in your workplace.

LIMITATIONS OF READABILITY TESTS

- It is possible to "doctor" an unclear text to get a good grade-level score and still have a difficult text.
- A readability test does not reflect the needs of the reader.
- The grade level a person has reached is not always a measure of her or his reading abilities.
- Readability tools can give you a general idea of the problem, but they cannot tell you exactly where the problem is.
- A readability tool can give you a false sense of security.

HOW TO USE THE SMOG (SIMPLE MEASURE OF GOBBLEDEGOOK) READABILITY FORMULA

If the text has more than 30 sentences:

1. Count off 30 sentences within the document: 10 consecutive sentences at the beginning, in the middle, and near the end of the text. Skip titles and headings; use only text.
2. Mark all polysyllabic words (words of three syllables or more) in the 30-sentence sample.
3. Total the number of these words.
4. Find the nearest square root of this total.
5. Add a constant of three to the square root. This is the reading level required to understand the text.

If the text has fewer than 30 sentences:

1. Count all words of three syllables or more in the text.
2. Count the number of sentences.
3. Find the average number of polysyllabic words per sentence:

   Average = Total number of polysyllabic words per sentence...divided by...total number of sentences

4. Subtract the total number of sentences from 30 and multiply the remainder by the average number of polysyllabic words per sentence.
5. Add this figure to the total number of polysyllabic words.
6. Find the nearest square root and add the constant of 3. This is the reading level required to understand the text

ADDITIONAL GUIDELINES FOR USING THE SMOG

- Hyphenated words are considered one word.
- Numbers printed as numerals should be pronounced to determine whether they are polysyllabic (e.g., 337 has seven syllables—or eight if you throw in "and").
- Proper nouns, if polysyllabic, should be counted too.
- Abbreviations should be pronounced in full to determine whether they are polysyllabic (e.g., ON, for Ontario, has four syllables).
- Include all repetitions of the same word, no matter how often it is used.
- The grade level is accurate to within 1.5 grades in either direction.

Field testing is a critical step that helps determine whether materials are written clearly. It is also an opportunity for others to discuss and evaluate your work.

It is quite easy to ask a coworker to review the clarity of your work. Develop a buddy system with others to examine your writing.

Focus groups are another way to perform a field test. Ask group members to comment on how easy it was to read your materials from a clear language and document design perspective.

DOCUMENT DESIGN

The appearance of a document can influence people to read it. If it is attractive, people will be more inclined to read further. However, excessive or inappropriate use of typestyles, fonts and features can be very distracting.

FORMATTING THE PAGE

Justified Margins

Justified text has a straight margin on the right as well as the left side of the page. Unless you select the type size and line length carefully, it may be harder to read because there can be too much space between words.

Centred Text

Placing titles and headings at the centre of the page is fine.
You should not, however, centre text because
this makes it harder for readers
to find the beginning of each line.

Flush Left

As a rule, this is the easiest format to read. The spaces between words are all the same, and readers are able to move easily from one line to the next.

SOME GUIDELINES FOR FORMATTING

Spacing

- Double space between lines whenever possible. The more white space, the easier your page is to read.
- If the lines are single-spaced, use a double space between paragraphs.
- When using bullets, don't place a semicolon at the end. They are unnecessary and may confuse the reader.
- Avoid using columns, especially narrow, justified ones.
- Use block style for memos and letters: no centred text—all text runs from the same margin, left to right.
- Indent important information only.
- Use a second page if necessary, rather than cramming too much text onto one page.

SOME GUIDELINES FOR SELECTING FONTS

- A serif typeface (such as the face used to set this book—one that has a short cross line at the end of the main strokes of letters) is easier to read than a sans serif face (one that doesn't have these lines).
- Try not to use more than one or two fonts in a piece of text.
- If possible, use at least a 12-point font, larger for overheads.
- Make sure the italics are not smaller than the standard fonts.
- Watch out for typefaces that are too ornate. They are harder to read.

SOME GUIDELINES FOR SELECTING FEATURES

- Try not to use too many features within a given text.
- Avoid block- or upper-case style for text. When words are printed entirely in capital letters, they lose their shape and are harder to read. You may, of course, type headings in upper-case letters.
- When underlining, be sure that the underline does not obscure the text. If used occasionally, this can be an effective way of highlighting information.
- Complete your document before you begin to add features and formatting.
- Be consistent with the features you choose for headings.

SUMMARY

By paying close attention to the principles of clear language and document design, organizations can help meet the literacy needs of employees. However, using clear language is not a substitute for workplace literacy education. Clear language must be integrated into an organization as a supplemental literacy training tool. Ultimately, following the basic principles involved in using clear language will contribute to effective communication so that all employees will benefit.

CHAPTER 13 # Evaluation: The Experience of One Hospital

by Angela Gillis

The Victoria General Hospital is a 640-bed referral centre for the Maritime provinces located in Halifax, Nova Scotia. The hospital has approximately 3,500 employees. Until 1990, training opportunities were targeted at professional staff. The first workplace education program was held in 1990 and was supported by the provincial department of education. The first hospital-based program in the province, it was piloted in the food and nutrition services department with six participants. In its second year, the program was expanded to the entire hospital and enrolment grew to 34. In 1992, the program became self-supporting and was expanded to include a volunteer tutor program. In 1993, an English as a second language option was added and short workshops on memo writing and computer training were introduced on a trial basis.

Enrolment in the program is holding steady at about 30 participants a year. Participation is voluntary and the progress of individuals is confidential. The goals of the program are to enable participants to develop self-esteem, and the reading, writing, oral English and math skills needed to solve problems they identify themselves. The program is geared to helping people with basic skills as well as those who wish to prepare for high school equivalency exams. Group sessions are provided by a paid workplace instructor and trained volunteer tutors are available to work individually with participants. The workplace instructor co-ordinates the volunteer tutor program.

A project team provides support and direction to the workplace instructor. Its membership consists of the workplace instructor, tutors, previous and current participants, managers, union representatives and the hospital co-ordinator of the program. Two workplace educators from the provincial department of education have acted as consultants to the project team. The team meets monthly to discuss issues relating to the workplace program, such as promotion, scheduling, availability of resources and program evaluation.

PROGRAM EVALUATION

Because the program is funded on a year-to-year basis, the project team became concerned that senior management would divert at least a share of the money that was being used for workplace education to other programs that also required funding. As a result, we decided to prepare ourselves for this possibility. We wanted to be able to demonstrate why the workplace education program deserved continued funding at the same level. At our initial meeting to develop a plan of action, we decided that our intention was to evaluate the program, not the progress of the participants. This decision guided the evaluation effort.

To tackle the issue of evaluating the program, we struck a working group of interested people from the project team membership. The group included the program instructor, two managers, a past participant, a union representative and me, the hospital co-ordinator of the program. Two workplace educators from the provincial education department acted as observers because they were interested in learning about the evaluation process. They were also helpful resources to the team.

Initially, the evaluation team possessed a great deal of enthusiasm but not much in the way of expertise. We held several meetings to plan the evaluation effort, but were hindered by a lack of confidence in our own decisions. For advice, we decided to contact ABC CANADA, a non-profit organization that focuses on promoting workplace education and training in the private sector.

Fortunately, our efforts at evaluation were happening at the same time as ABC CANADA was developing a guide to evaluating workplace education programs. While we needed help with the evaluation process, ABC staff was looking for sites to try out their evaluation guide. As a result, during the evaluation project, we were able to schedule three days of workshops facilitated by Sue Folinsbee of ABC CANADA and Paul Jurmo of Literacy Partnerships, a private consulting firm based in Brunswick, New Jersey. They helped us define what it was we wanted to know, what questions would give us the information we were seeking, and how best to collect the data.

TEAM APPROACH TO EVALUATION

Our first job was to decide what we wanted to learn from the evaluation, by far the most difficult task of the whole endeavour. It required us to think about why we were evaluating the program and what we wanted to learn. We decided that we had three goals:

- To document the information needed to support future funding.
- To document the accomplishments of the program.
- To determine how to improve the program.

We grappled with issues of confidentiality and testing, eventually deciding that we were not willing to test participants to measure individual progress. Because our program was based on adult education principles, we felt that academic criteria were an unsuitable evaluation tool. Within the program, each learner identified individual goals and set out to achieve them in the way best-suited to her or him. There was no obligation to pass an exam or obtain a grade at the end of the program: success was defined by the learner. We felt that a broader approach to evaluation was needed to determine the value of the program. As a result, after some discussion, we ended up with four evaluation questions:

- What have been the goals of the program?
- What has been accomplished to date?
- Should the program be continued and why?
- What actions need to be taken to improve and expand the program?

THE PROCESS

The next step was to decide who would be able to answer these questions. We knew that we needed a variety of perspectives. Once again, it took some discussion, but we came up with a list of stakeholders that we felt we needed to hear from. Although it is always tempting to talk to your supporters, we also wanted to learn what those who didn't support us thought so that we could develop a strategy for winning their support.

The first list we came up with was complete—and very long. Once we reminded ourselves that we had to be able to complete the work ourselves, we found it much easier to narrow down the list to the key players. The final list included current and past learners, learners who left the program, tutors, education staff, managers and supervisors and the members of the project team.

Our next task was to determine how to collect the information. At this point, the group found it much easier to make decisions. We had a clearly stated purpose, a list of key stakeholders and the questions they needed to be asked. We decided to use a variety of means to collect the data because the availability of the key players varied. The past and present participants were not usually free to leave their worksite, although current participants met in class twice weekly. The schedules of the managers and supervisors were more flexible, but also very demanding. Because the project team met monthly, it was convenient to meet with its members as a group.

The data collection methods included face-to-face interviews, telephone interviews, focus groups and questionnaires. The four evaluation questions were phrased appropriately for each group of stakeholders and the same questions were asked of all members of each group. To maintain as much objectivity as possible, interviewers were assigned. We also requested the assistance of additional facilitators to conduct focus groups for us. The group decided that everyone would share the work of collecting the data and that the workplace education instructor would be responsible for writing the final report. It took three weeks to collect the data. From conception to final report, the entire evaluation process took six months.

SUMMARY OF EVALUATION RESULTS

Question 1: What have been the goals of the program?

The goals of the workplace education program are to enable participants to develop self-esteem and the reading, writing, oral English and math skills needed to solve problems they identify themselves. We learned that most participants had a clear understanding of the program goals. However, some supervisors were unclear about the meaning of workplace education and how they could support the participants from their area.

Question 2: What has been accomplished to date?

We learned that a wide range of benefits was associated with the program. Most learners felt they had achieved their personal goals. Those who hadn't yet met their goals expected to do so through the next program. In addition, many participants felt that they had increased self-confidence and self-esteem. Others surveyed reported an increase in morale and participation at the workplace. The tutors, most of whom were hospital employees, also felt that they had increased their self-confidence and gained skills that could be transferred to their own jobs.

We also became aware of some concerns about the program. Some supervisors were concerned about the stress that participants were under, difficulties in arranging schedules and imbalances in workload because participants needed release time to attend classes. Our confidentiality policy created confusion for some supervisors. This related to issues involving knowledge of an employee's participation in the program, which was withheld only at the request of a participant, as well as knowledge of an employee's goals and progress. Some supervisors felt that the limits on the information they were provided affected the support they were able to offer.

Question 3: Should the program be continued and why?

We were very pleased to learn that everyone felt strongly that the program should be continued. They believed that skills gained from the program enabled staff to deal with the demands of the workplace as well as those of their personal lives.

Question 4: What actions need to be taken to improve and expand the program?

A long list of recommendations was developed from the responses to this question. We were told to continue doing many things. The instructors' skills and approach to learning were rated very highly by the participants. Holding the classes on site at a time convenient for the most common shifts was very important to the participants. The fact that the hospital funded the program and provided release time to attend classes emphasized to the participants that the program was considered important.

Many of the suggested improvements were implemented before the next program started, only weeks after the evaluation was completed. Other recommendations were more complex and took more time to achieve. However, all recommendations were addressed.

Here are the 10 major recommendations:

- Schedule all classes in the same room.
- Increase the instructors' time.
- Offer more flexibility in class times.
- Give supervisors at least two weeks' notice of class schedules in order to comply with union contract requirements.
- Improve communication with supervisors about the program.
- Develop clear confidentiality guidelines.
- Propose a hospital policy to cover the 50-50 release time.
- Develop a handbook outlining the purpose and practices of the workplace education program.
- Provide workshops in specific areas (i.e., memo writing, telephone skills, public speaking, report writing).
- Include computer training.

HOW THE REPORT HAS BEEN USED TO DATE

The evaluation report has provided us with direction and has become a roadmap for the program. It helped to orient the next instructor and was invaluable in providing support for special requests such as room scheduling.

THE BENEFITS OF COMPLETING THE EVALUATION

We're very confident now that the program is meeting the needs of the participants and we have a clear vision for the future of the program. We are prepared for funding to be challenged, although this has not happened. Each team member can take back to the workplace the experience gained in evaluation. The project enhanced our visibility and gave us internal and external recognition.

WHAT WE'D DO DIFFERENTLY NEXT TIME

As we see more and more benefits to the program, our commitment to workplace education has strengthened over the years. If I had the chance to start such a program again I would channel more resources into gaining support from the direct supervisors of potential participants. The value of this support should not be underestimated. Although the support of senior management is critical, the program's success is also very much affected by support at the grass-roots level. We initially expected participants to act as the liaison between the program and the supervisor. However, this approach did not work successfully and we learned that it was important for the instructor to speak directly with supervisors.

One change I would strongly suggest to others attempting to evaluate their program is to take the time to develop a plan for a follow-up evaluation during the planning for the initial evaluation. Because of staff changes and layoffs, more than half the members of the evaluation team are no longer available. It will require much more energy to start over than it would have required for us to carry out a predetermined plan.

THE FINAL WORD

Initiating a workplace education program was the right thing to do. Completing the evaluation of the program validated this action and also gave us the information we needed to make the program even better. Our program is stronger and more secure as a result. Program evaluation is a very important activity and well worth the effort.

Bibliography

REFERENCES

Arnold, R., B. Burke, C. James, D. Martin & B. Thomas. *Educating for a Change*. Toronto: Between the Lines/Doris Marshall Institute, 1991.

Auerbach, E.R. & N. Wallerstein. *ESL for Action: Problem-Posing at the Workplace*. Reading, Mass.: Addison-Wesley, 1987.

Barndt, D., M.E. Belfiore & J. Handscombe. *English at Work: A Tool Kit for Teachers*. Syracuse, N.Y.: New Readers Press, 1991.

Barndt, D., F. Cristall & D. Marino. *Getting There: Producing Photostories with Immigrant Women*. Toronto: Between the Lines, 1982.

Belfiore, M.E. "The Changing World of Work Research Project." In *TESL Talk*. Vol. 21: 1993.

Bell, J. *Teaching Multilevel Classes in ESL*. Los Angeles: Dominie Press, 1988.

Bell, J. "The Levi-Strauss Project: Development of a Curriculum." In *TESL Talk*. Vol. 13, no. 4: 1982.

Bell, J. & B. Burnaby. *A Handbook for ESL Literacy*. Toronto: OISE Press/Hodder & Stoughton, 1984.

British Columbia Ministry of Education. *English for Work*. Vancouver: British Columbia Ministry of Education, 1982.

Elver, L., T. Goldstein, J. McDonald & J. Reid. *Improving Intercultural Communication in the Workplace: An Approach to Needs Assessment*. Toronto: Board of Education for the City of Toronto/Ontario Ministry of Citizenship, 1986.

Folinsbee, S. *An Organizational Approach to Workplace Basic Skills: A Guidebook for Literacy Practitioners*. Ottawa: Young Men's and Young Women's Christian Association, 1992.

Gaston, J. *Cultural Awareness Teaching Techniques*. Brattleboro: Oro Lingua Associates, 1984.

Goldstein, T. "The ESL Community and the Changing World of Work." In *TESL Talk*. Vol. 21: 1993.

Gubbay, D. *Role-Play: The Theory and Process of a Method for Increasing Language Awareness*. Southall, Middlesex: National Council for Industrial Language Training, 1980.

Kirby, S. & K. McKenna. *Experience, Research, Social Change: Methods from the Margins*. Toronto: Garamond Press, 1989.

Spradley, J. *The Ethnographic Interview*. New York: Holt, Rinehart and Winston, 1979.

Taylor, M. & G. Lewe. *Basic Skills Training: A Launchpad for Success in the Workplace*. Ottawa: Algonquin College, 1990.

Taylor, M.L. "The Language Experience Approach." In *Approaches to Adult ESL Literacy Instruction* (J. Crandall & J. Kreeft Peyton, Eds.). Washington, D.C.: Center for Applied Linguistics/Delta Systems, 1993.

Turk, J. & J. Unda. "So We Can Make Our Voices Heard: The Ontario Federation of Labour's BEST Project on Worker Literacy." In *Basic Skills for the Workplace* (M. Taylor, G. Lewe & J. Draper, Eds.). Toronto: Culture Concepts, 1991.

CLASSROOM MATERIALS

Alberta Vocational College. *From the Classroom to the Workplace: Training Workplace Trainers*. Edmonton: Alberta Vocational College, 1994 (Facilitator's manual, participant's manual, handouts, overheads and video).

Auerbach, E.R. & N. Wallerstein. *ESL for Action: Problem-Posing at the Workplace*. Reading, Mass.: Addison-Wesley, 1987.

Balliro, L. *Workplays: You and Your Rights on the Job* and *Workbook for Workplays: You and Your Rights on the Job*. Video & manual. North Dartmouth, Mass.: Labor Education Center, Southeastern Massachusetts University, 1988.

Barndt, D., F. Cristall & D. Marino. *Getting There: Producing Photostories with Immigrant Women*. Toronto: Between the Lines, 1982.

Barndt, D., M.E. Belfiore & J. Handscombe. *English at Work: A Tool Kit for Teachers*. Syracuse, N.Y.: New Readers Press, 1991.

Board of Education for the City of Toronto. *We Make the Clothes*. Toronto: Learnxs Press, 1985.

Bond, J. & T. McGill. *Paperwork Plus: Literacy Materials for the Service Industry, Hotel Edition*. Etobicoke, Ont.: Etobicoke Board of Education, MWP, 1994.

Gumperz, J., T.C. Jupp & C. Roberts. *Crosstalk*. Southall, Middlesex: The National Centre for Industrial Language Training, 1979.

Grotsky, R. *Basic Skills Training for Small Business: The Subway Franchise Model*. Toronto: Praxis Training and Skills Development, 1992.

Hemmendinger, A., R. Wehlau, K. Dehli, G. Dobbs, P. Dwyer, D. Hilton, J. Horsman & C. Ingram. *This Is Not a Test: A Kit for New Readers*. Toronto: East End Literacy Press, 1990.

LeForestier, D. *Personal Assessment Process*. Thornbury, Ont.: Georgian Learning Associates.

Metro Labour Education and Skills Training Centre. *Working in the Hospital*. Toronto: Metro Labour Education and Skills Training Centre, 1990.

Mottershead, J. & P. Erickson. *Job Effectiveness Training Curriculum*. Edmonton: Alberta Vocational College, 1989.

Plaizier, H. *The English of Personal Care Work: A Workbook*. Edmonton: English Language Professionals, 1994.

Reid, J., E. Taborek, L. Elver, F. Winer, D. Woo & W.N. Villano. *English for the Fashion Industry*. Toronto: Board of Education for the City of Toronto, 1986.

Sauvé, V., J. Nicholls & L. Crawford. *Time for the Basics*. Edmonton: English Language Professionals, 1991.

Sauvé, V., B. Warner & P. Malinowski. *The English Shift: A Workbook for New Canadian Hospital Support Workers*. Englewood Cliffs, N.J.: Prentice Hall, 1994.

Toronto Workers Health and Safety Legal Clinic. *ESL Instructors' Guide to Health and Safety in the Workplace*. Toronto: Toronto Workers Health and Safety Legal Clinic, 1993.

Yates, V., E. Christmas & P. Wilson. *Cross-Cultural Training: Developing Skills and Awareness in Communication*. Southall, Middlesex: The National Centre for Industrial Language Training, 1982.

BOOKS AND ARTICLES OF INTEREST TO WORKPLACE TEACHERS

GENERAL INTEREST

Arnold, R., B. Burke, C. James, D. Martin & B. Thomas. *Educating for a Change*. Toronto: Between the Lines/Doris Marshall Institute, 1991.

Askov, E., B. Aderman & N. Hemmelstein. *Upgrading Basic Skills for the Workplace*. University Park, Pennsylvania: Institute for the Study of Adult Literacy, College of Education, Pennsylvania State University/Pennsylvania Coalition for Adult Literacy, 1989.

Auerbach, E. *Making Meaning, Making Change: Participatory Curriculum Development for Adult ESL*. Washington, D.C.: Center for Applied Linguistics, 1992.

Baldwin, R. *Clear Writing and Literacy*. Toronto: Ontario Literacy Coalition, 1990.

Bell, J. "The Levi Strauss Project: Development of a Curriculum." In *TESL Talk*. Vol. 13, no. 4: 1982

Bell, J. *Teaching Multilevel Classes in ESL*. Los Angeles: Dominie Press, 1988.

Bell, J. & B. Burnaby. *A Handbook for ESL Literacy*. Toronto: OISE Press/Hodder & Stoughton, 1984.

Brand, M., A. Gallaugher & D. Langevin. *I Can Do the Job Very Well: A Collection of Job Search Stories by Adult ESL Learners*. Toronto: Board of Education for the City of Toronto, Continuing Education Department, 1992.

British Columbia Ministry of Education. *English for Work*. Vancouver: British Columbia Ministry of Education, 1982.

Business Council for Effective Literacy. "Job-Related Basic Skills: A Guide for Planners of Employee Programs." In *BCEL Bulletin*. Vol. 2: 1987.

Canadian Farmworkers Union. *A Time to Learn: An ESL Course for the Canadian Farmworkers Union*. Burnaby, B.C.: Canadian Farmworkers Union, 1983.

Carnevale, A., L. Gainer & A. Meltzer. *Workplace Basics: The Skills Employers Want*. Alexandria, Va.: The American Society for Training and Development/United States Department of Labor, 1988.

Carnavale, A., L. Gainer & A. Meltzer. *Workplace Basics Training Manual*. San Francisco: Jossey-Bass, 1990.

Crandall, J. & J. Kreeft Peyton (Eds.). *Approaches to Adult ESL Literacy Instruction*. Washington, D.C., & McHenry, Ill.: Center for Applied Linguistics/Delta Systems, 1993.

Elver, L., T. Goldstein, J. McDonald & J. Reid. *Improving Intercultural Communication in the Workplace: An Approach to Needs Assessment*. Toronto: Board of Education for the City of Toronto/Ontario Ministry of Citizenship, 1986.

Fingeret, H.A., A. Tom, P. Dyer, A. Morley, J. Dawson, L. Harper, D. Lee, M. McCue & M. Niks. *Lives of Change: An Ethnographic Evaluation of Two Learner-Centred Literacy Programs*. Vancouver: Invergarry Adult Learning Centre/Vancouver Municipal Workplace Language Program, 1994.

Folinsbee, S. & P. Jurmo. *Collaborative Evaluation: A Handbook for Workplace Development Planners*. Toronto: ABC Canada, 1994.

Folinsbee, S. & P. Jurmo. *Collaborative Workplace Development: An Overview*. Toronto: ABC Canada, 1994.

Folinsbee, S. *Guidelines for Implementing Multicultural Workplace Programs and Redesigning Tailor-Made Intercultural/Race Relations Training Programs for the Workplace*. Toronto: George Brown College, 1989.

Folinsbee, S. *An Organizational Approach to Workplace Basic Skills: A Guidebook for Literacy Practitioners* Ottawa: Young Men's and Young Women's Christian Association, 1992.

Freeman, M. & A. Husain. *Multicultural Management: Starting with Orientation*. North York, Ont.: CORE Foundation, 1989.

Gowen, S. G. *The Politics of Workplace Literacy*. New York: Teachers College Press, 1992.

Gubbay, D. *Role-Play: The Theory and Process of a Method for Increasing Language Awareness*. Southall, Middlesex: The National Council for Industrial Language Training, 1980.

Holt, M. & J. Bell. *Improving Communication in Multicultural Workplaces: An Evaluation Manual for EWP Instructors*. Toronto: Ontario Institute for Studies in Education, 1987.

Imel, S. & S. Kerka. *Workplace Literacy: A Guide to the Literature and Resources*. Columbus, Ohio: Center on Education and Training for Employment, Ohio State University, 1992.

Jenkinson, J. & C. Ramkhalawansingh. *Clear Language and Design*. Toronto: City of Toronto, 1990.

Kainola, M.A. *Making Changes*. Toronto: Cross Cultural Communication Centre, 1982.

Karassik, J.W. *Literacy and Learning Disabilities: A Handbook for Literacy Workers*. Ottawa: Learning Disabilities Association of Canada, 1989.

Klassen, C. & J. Robinson. *An Approach to ESL Literacy Assessment*. Victoria, B.C.: Ministry of Advanced Education, 1992.

Linked Skills Working Party. *Linked Skills: A Handbook for Skills and ESL Tutors*. Cambridge, Mass.: National Extension College, 1983.

Lam, C., A. Whittington, M. Adamczyk, K. Rine, J. Murray & W. Thompson. *The MWP Process: A Developer's Guide*. Toronto: Board of Education for the City of Toronto, 1990.

Lund, B. "The ESL Program at Jantzen of Canada Ltd.: An Evaluation." In *TESL Talk*. Vol. 13, no. 4: 1982.

McCaskell, T. *Camp: Multicultural/Multiracial Residential Camp for Secondary School Students*. Toronto: Board of Education for the City of Toronto, 1988.

McCaskell, T. *World History of Racism in Minutes*. Toronto: Board of Education for the City of Toronto, 1986.

McGrail, L. *Teaching and Learning from Strengths: ESL Tutor Training Curriculum Guide*. Boston: Adult Literacy Resource Institute, University of Massachusetts/Roxbury Community College, 1990.

Multiculturalism and Citizenship, Canada. *Plain Language: Clear and Simple*. Ottawa: Supply and Services Canada, 1991.

Nash, A., A. Cason, M. Rhum, L. McGrail & R. Gomez-Sanford. *Talking Shop: A Curriculum Sourcebook for Participatory Adult ESL*. Washington, D.C.: Center for Applied Linguistics, 1992

Nore, G.W.E. *Clear Lines: How to Compose and Design Clear Language Documents for the Workplace*. Toronto: Frontier College Press, 1991.

Ontario Ministry of Skills Development. *How to Set Up Literacy and Basic Skills Training in the Workplace*. Toronto: Ontario Ministry of Skills Development, 1989.

Plett, L. *Workplace Instructor's Handbook*. Winnipeg: Literacy Workers Alliance of Manitoba, 1994.

Podoliak, E. (Ed.). "ESL in the Changing World of Work." Theme issue of *TESL Talk*. Vol. 21: 1993.

Reid, J., E. Adamowski & M. Brand. *Getting Started: A Handbook for Volunteer ESL Instructors and Their Supervisors*. Toronto: Board of Education for the City of Toronto, 1988.

Roberts, C., E. Davies & T. Jupp. *Language and Discrimination: A Study of Communication in Multi-Ethnic Workplaces*. London: Longman, 1992.

Sarmiento, A.R. & A. Kay. *Worker-Centered Learning: A Union Guide to Workplace Literacy*. Washington D.C.: AFL-CIO Human Resources Development Institute, 1990.

Scott, C.D. & D.T. Jaffe. *Managing Organizational Change: A Practical Guide for Managers*. Menlo Park, Calif.: Crisp Publications, 1989.

Shore, S., A. Black, A. Simpson & M. Coombe. *Positively Different: Guidance for Developing Inclusive Adult Literacy, Language and Numeracy Curricula*. Canberra, Australia: Department of Employment, Education and Training, 1993.

Taylor, M. & G. Lewe. *Basic Skills Training: A Launchpad for Success in the Workplace*. Ottawa: Algonquin College, 1990.

Taylor, M. & J. Draper (Eds.). *Basic Skills for the Workplace*. Toronto: Culture Concepts, 1991.

Wallerstein, N. *Language and Culture in Conflict*. Reading, Mass.: Addison-Wesley, 1983.

Tom, A., H.A. Fingeret, M. Niks, J. Dawson, P. Dyer, L. Harper, D. Lee, M. McCue & A. Morley. *Suspended in a Web of Relationships: Collaborative Ethnographic Evaluation*. Vancouver: Invergarry Adult Learning Centre/Vancouver Municipal Workplace Language Program, 1994.

ANTI-RACISM EDUCATION

Beck, C. *Better Schools: A Values Perspective*. New York: Falmer Press, 1990.

Belfiore, M.E. "The Changing World of Work Research Project." In *TESL Talk*. Vol. 21: 1993.

Goldstein, T. "The ESL Community and the Changing World of Work." In *TESL Talk*. Vol. 21: 1993.

Henry, F. & E. Ginzberg. *Who Gets the Work? A Test for Racial Discrimination in Employment*. Toronto: Urban Alliance on Race Relations, 1985.

Husain, A. *Multicultural Management: Starting with Orientation*. North York, Ont.: CORE Foundation, 1989.

Kozol, J. *Savage Inequalities: Children in America's Schools*. New York: Crown, 1991.

Kunjufu, J. *Countering the Conspiracy to Destroy Black Boys*. Chicago: African American Images, 1985.

Lee, E. *Letters to Marcia: A Teacher's Guide to Anti-Racist Education*. Toronto: Cross Cultural Communication Centre, 1985.

Lee, E. with J. Shields. "Displacement and Discrimination: A Double Burden for Workers of Colour." In *TESL Talk*. Vol. 21: 1993.

Thomas, B. & C. Novogrodsky. *Combatting Racism in the Workplace: A Course for Workers and Readings Kit*. Toronto: Cross Cultural Communication Centre, 1983.

Thompson, W., V.R. Smith, A. Mukherjee & B. D'Antini. *Anti-Racist Education and the Adult Learner: A Handbook for Educators in Adult and Continuing Education Programs*. Toronto: Board of Education for the City of Toronto, 1991.

ORGANIZATIONAL NEEDS ASSESSMENTS

Askov, E., B. Aderman & N. Hemmelstein. *Upgrading Basic Skills for the Workplace*. University Park, Pa.: Institute for the Study of Adult Literacy, College of Education, University of Pennsylvania/Pennsylvania Coalition for Adult Literacy, 1989.

Business Council for Effective Literacy. "Job-Related Basic Skills: A Guide for Planners of Employee Programs." In *BCEL Bulletin*. Vol. 2: 1987.

Carnevale, A., L. Gainer & A. Meltzer. *Workplace Basics: The Skills Employers Want*. Alexandria, Va.: American Society for Training and Development/United States Department of Labor, 1988.

Elver, L, T. Goldstein, J. MacDonald & J. Reid. *Improving Intercultural Communication in the Workplace: An Approach to Needs Assessment*. Toronto: Board of Education for the City of Toronto/Ontario Ministry of Citizenship, 1986.

Folinsbee, S. & P. Jurmo. *Collaborative Needs Assessment: A Handbook for Workplace Development Planners*. Toronto: ABC Canada, 1994.

Ontario Ministry of Skills Development. *How to Set Up Literacy and Basic Skills Training in the Workplace*. Toronto: Ontario Ministry of Skills Development, 1989.

Sarmiento, A. "Workplace Literacy and Workplace Politics." In *Work America*. Vol. 6, no. 9: 1989.

Spradley, J. *The Ethnographic Interview*. New York: Holt, Rinehart and Winston, 1979.

About the Contributors

KATHLEEN FLANAGAN is a doctoral candidate in the adult education department of the Ontario Institute for Studies in Education. A specialist in photography and cultural studies, she produced an anti-racist program, titled "part of the Solution," for use at a Halifax elementary school.

SUE (WAUGH) FOLINSBEE is director of workplace education for ABC CANADA, with responsibility for developing and maintaining the organization's workplace advisory service. The author of several documents on workplace basic skills education, she has a special interest in developing and refining new evaluation tools for collaborative workplace basic skills programs.

CORINNA FRATTINI is a workplace literacy trainer at Frontier College. She consults with companies interested in workplace literacy and delivers training in the area of clear language and the design and implementation of workplace learning programs.

ANGELA GILLIS provides training and development for dietary staff in a large hospital in Nova Scotia. She initiated the first hospital-based workplace education program in Nova Scotia.

CHRISTINA PIKIOS is co-ordinator and consultant at the Intercultural Training and Resource Centre in Continuing Studies at the University of British Columbia. In partnership with university faculties and private and public organizations, she designs and delivers programs in intercultural communication.

VIRGINIA SAUVÉ is an Alberta educator well-known for her work in participatory education, workplace education and ESL literacy. She runs a private company, English Language Professionals, and has taught English as a second language at two Canadian universities.